Expanded Praise fo

"The experience and insights Bill and Casey bring to the table are unmatched. They're not just attorneys; they're also strategic advisors who deeply understand the business of dentistry and have tenaciously advanced Riverside Oral Surgery's interests through a decade of significant growth. Whether I'm dealing with a high-stakes transaction, a regulatory question, an operational issue, or anything in between, I know I have the right legal team by my side."

- Jason Auerbach, DDS, Founder, Riverside Oral Surgery / @BloodyToothGuy

"Bill and Casey successfully guided me through the creation of a personal DSO, and they have been an integral part of my team ever since. Over the years, we have executed a wide range of transactions, including multiple practice acquisitions and real estate purchases, the sale of a minority interest in the DSO to a strategic partner, and the creation of operating agreements that are truly win-win for my partners and myself. Not only are they exceptional attorneys, but they share my entrepreneurial mindset and are always there to guide me to the right outcome."

- Curtis S. Crandall, Founder & COO, Cranco Dentistry, LLC

"Bill and Casey's acumen in the DSO space is second to none! Their relationships within the profession, their vast experience with negotiations and closings, and their ability to shepherd dentists through the transition process will give comfort to anyone venturing into the DSO arena."
- Glenn Gorab, DMD, Founder, Clifton Oral and Maxillofacial Surgery, P.A.

"Strong opinions exist on all sides of the DSO movement, but *The DSO Decision* presents the facts in a clear and unbiased way. This book couldn't have come at a better time in the profession, and no matter what angle you're coming from, you'll certainly benefit from Bill and Casey's wisdom."
- Ben R. Johnson, DMD, Owner, Pacific Northwest Oral and Maxillofacial Surgeons

Practicing Dentists – Scan and Receive Your Free Audiobooks Today!

Pain Free Dental Deals

The DSO Decision

THE
DSO
DECISION

WINNING ANSWERS FROM EVERY ANGLE

WILLIAM S.
BARRETT
AND CASEY
GOCEL

Published by Redwood Publishing, LLC
Orange County, California
www.redwooddigitalpublishing.com

ISBN 978-1-956470-05-5 (hardcover)

ISBN 978-1-956470-06-2 (ebook)

Cover design by Michelle Manley of Graphique Designs, LLC
Book design and production by Jose Pepito and Redwood Publishing, LLC
Editing by Sissi Haner

CONTENTS

INTRODUCTION

In the dental profession today, it is nearly impossible to get through a conversation without broaching the topic of DSOs. There is a lot of information out there, both true and false, and there is also a great deal of confusion about what DSOs really do and how they operate. There is even confusion surrounding the acronym. What does "DSO" stand for? DSO is used in the industry both as "dental service organization" or "dental support organization," but what does that mean? More importantly, what is the impact of DSOs on the future of the dental professional?

This book is for anyone who is thinking of selling their practice to a DSO, partnering with a DSO, starting a DSO, working for a DSO, or just looking for a better understanding of how DSOs operate. This book is also beneficial for anyone looking for an effective strategy to compete with DSOs in the quest for the preservation of private practice dentistry.

While we cannot predict the future precisely, we can tell you that the impact on the dental industry will be profound.

DSOs continue to be the fastest-growing segment of dentistry, with no end in sight.

We thought it would be helpful to give you the origins of the DSO model and what it has evolved into. There are a variety of business models, partly because DSOs are governed by a host of regulations that vary from state to state. There are also a wide range of business models that work within those legal frameworks.

This book is designed to be a resource without judgment. We want to give you the good, the bad, and the ugly. Our goals are to provide a realistic picture of what is involved in selling to, or partnering with, a DSO, outline the methods and challenges of starting your own DSO, and dispel some of the myths and misconceptions about the model.

As co-chairs of the National Dental Law Center at Mandelbaum Barrett, we have formed and represented countless DSOs throughout the United States. Each one is different. There are complexities not apparent to the outside world, and the legal and structural requirements of DSOs are distinctly different from an owner-managed dental practice.

Like them or not, DSOs are here to stay. Our goal is to give you some much-needed clarity and insight into how DSOs operate. We will do a deep dive into the world of DSOs and, later in this book, will also present strategies for your business if you are looking to work with DSOs or remain independent and compete effectively.

CHAPTER ONE

Understanding DSOs

WHAT IS A DSO?

DSOs are essentially dental practice management companies that provide most, if not all, of the non-clinical functions of a practice, including human resources, accounting, billing, leasing, marketing, payroll, purchasing, IT, regulatory compliance, and legal. In essence, they manage the business around a practicing dentist. In many cases, the DSO owns or leases the real estate and all of the equipment for the practice. Most of the time, all non-clinical employees (i.e., everyone other than the doctors, and in some states, the hygienists and/or dental assistants) are employees of the DSO and not of the practice. DSOs range widely in size, supporting anywhere from two practices to hundreds of practices.

The one thing all DSOs have in common is that they centralize as many functions as possible to leverage economies of scale and maximize the use of fixed overhead to increase efficiency and profitability at the practice level.

The DSO industry is often referred to as the "corporate practice of dentistry." The reason for this is simple. As a non-licensed, non-professional entity, the creation of a DSO makes it possible for a non-dentist to participate in the ownership of (and share profits in) one or more dental practices. These non-dentist owners may be sophisticated investors (think private equity firms) or working partners who do not have a license to practice dentistry.

The challenge these investors face is that, in nearly every state, it is illegal for a non-dentist to "own" a dental practice. At the time of this writing, non-professionals are only permitted to invest and own equity in a dental practice in Arizona, Mississippi, New Mexico, North Dakota, Ohio, Pennsylvania, South Carolina, Utah, and Wisconsin. Notwithstanding, many of these states impose legal restrictions on how the non-professional holds the interest and what percentage of the practice the non-dentist can own.

A DSO, however, is not a dental practice. In most states, it does not own the patient lists or other clinical assets of the practice, and it does not employ the licensed dentists. Instead, a DSO is a management company, and in such capacity, there are no restrictions on its right to own a business. DSOs manage, and in most cases own, the non-clinical aspects of the practice. The dental practice contracts with the DSO to provide management services to the practice in exchange for a management fee. The specific nuances surrounding this split-ownership of the practice's assets (clinical vs. non-clinical) take many forms, in part because of the varied regulations governing DSOs in each state and because there is a wide range of business models that all work to achieve the goal.

One of the reasons DSOs are successful is that many dentists do not want to be burdened by the operational aspects of running a dental business. They simply want to focus on practicing dentistry. The DSO can create economies of scale with nearly every aspect of the dental practice operation, which can result in a more profitable business model.

When a DSO acquires the assets of a practice, most often the selling doctor becomes an employee of the practice and/ or a minority interest holder in the DSO. This is appealing to the dentist, as he or she will receive a substantial payment for the assets of the practice. They then will continue to work in the practice while earning fair market compensation without having to deal with the day-to-day headaches of management such as human resources, billing, collections, marketing, legal compliance, insurance carriers, negotiating lease renewals, and all of the other non-clinical elements of running the practice.

There is an ongoing debate about whether DSOs are beneficial to patients and the profession. We will not engage heavily in that debate in this book because we have found that, as in every industry, there are businesses where the customers—or patients, in this case—come out ahead, and everyone wins, and there are businesses where the benefits mostly inure to the owners. In other words, the DSO concept is neither good nor bad. The issues of how the DSO is modeled and implemented determine whether the patients will benefit. Remember, all DSOs are different, and the analysis as to patient benefit must be made on a case-by-case basis.

THE TWO BASIC MODELS: THIRD-PARTY DSOS AND PERSONAL DSOS

Essentially, there are two distinct models for DSOs. The first is what we will refer to as "third-party DSOs." These are organizations that are formed to acquire practices, with the assistance of a dentist partner, to provide operational services, usually with a significant amount of investment capital behind them.

The second is the "personal DSO." This is the model where a multi-location practice owner creates his or her own management company to take advantage of centralized management services needed by the practice, resulting in greater efficiency and minimization of overhead. This model often includes additional minority partners at the practice level and/or the management company level. The founder dentist often (but certainly not always) functions as the CEO of the management company.

If minority partners are involved, the owners will enter into a partnership agreement for the corporate governance of the DSO. The partnership agreement formalizes the relationship between the owners and their respective legal and economic rights.

The third-party DSO model differs from the personal DSO model in that the owners of the DSO are different than the owners of the practice entities under its management. Third-party DSOs generally require one or more "friendly dentists." The friendly dentist(s) owns the dental practice under management, and the third-party investors own the DSO entity. In many cases, the DSO will manage practices all over the country or throughout a particular region and will work with several friendly dentists who own the clinical practices under management.

A third-party DSO often relies on investment capital and/or bank debt, while a personal DSO model may be self-funded through personal cash flow or bank loans. The personal DSO model may eventually bring in outside in-vestors to fund growth as well. Once the founding dentist gives up majority control of his or her DSO, the corporate structure transitions to a third-party DSO model.

In either model, the DSO will be paid a manage-ment fee from the practice entities that it manages. This is most often a fixed monthly fee, plus reimbursement for out-of-pocket expenses. It is important to note that in many states, paying management fees to a DSO based on a percentage of profits (rather than a fixed dollar amount) violates state regulations governing the corporate practice of dentistry. Many individuals have been penalized for merely creating the appearance (even if not actually doing so) that they are withdrawing all the profits of the practice (thereby rendering the practice insolvent) and turning the dentist into a *de facto* employee. How the money flows and is managed is something that has come under great scrutiny and must be structured carefully to ensure compliance with state and federal healthcare regulatory laws.

In recent years, a handful of DSOs have emerged that do not actually acquire dental practices. Instead, they provide a wide range of *a la carte* services from which a participating dentist may select the specific management services needed for his or her practice. This is an excellent choice for a doctor who is not looking to sell his or her practice but still wants to outsource some or all management responsibilities. Services generally available on the "menu" include the typical third-party DSO services (i.e., human resources, payroll, call center, billing, marketing, equipment leasing, real estate management, lease negotiations, staff training, and accounting). The benefits of selecting such services include, but are not limited to, enhanced purchasing power, reduced benefit and insurance costs, and increased negotiated reimbursements from insurance providers.

Whether you are investing in a third-party DSO or thinking of starting your own personal DSO, navigating the DSO legal and regulatory landscape requires a substantial amount of legal work, ranging from the formation of the business, to negotiating the partnership agreement, to creating the various management services agreements between the DSO and the managed practices.

THE HISTORY OF DENTAL SERVICE ORGANIZATIONS

The history of DSOs can be traced all the way back to the 1930s when a doctor by the name of Robert F. Beauchamp acquired his father's California-based dental practice and subsequently opened a second practice. In 1939, California passed a regulation prohibiting an individual dentist from owning more than two practices. Before the law went into effect, Dr. Beauchamp seized the opportunity and used financing to acquire seven additional practices.

His business model focused on underserved communities, always offering financing for his care, thus creating the concept of a "credit dentist." He saw the value in branding the practices under a single name and owning the underlying real estate. Imitation followed in one form or another throughout the country over the ensuing decades.

Dr. Beauchamp also advertised, which made him a pariah in the dental community. He was not allowed to join the California Dental Association for many decades. Years later, his practices were acquired by a DSO that ultimately became Western Dental & Orthodontics, which now has more than 300 locations under management in multiple states.

This type of acquisition entity was initially referred to as a Dental Management Organization, or DMO. After years of legal challenges in various states, the DMOs realized that the term "management" implied more control than most dental societies would tolerate. Often, state dental societies worked and lobbied furiously to pass legislation to limit the power of such organizations or to make their existence illegal, with some level of success.

Eventually, the phrase "dental service organization" emerged, although sometimes the entity was referred to as a dental support organization. This re-branding of DMOs to DSOs was an attempt to make these organizations look less "corporate." Regardless of the name, such management companies figured out a way to lawfully control dental practices, which made them the *de facto* owners of the practices.

The primary concern of dental societies and associations throughout the country was the belief that these DSOs were telling their dentists how to practice dentistry and were controlling clinical patient care. The fear was justified, as discussed in the Aspen Dental case detailed in chapter 8. At the time, many DSOs were pushing their dentists to "sell" certain procedures in order to meet production goals. Today, however, DSOs must take a hands-off approach to the clinical side of the practices they manage, except to provide advanced training in group sessions to their participating dentists. The licensed doctor must have authority over all clinical decisions and with respect to patient care.

DSOs can still provide significant value in managing the non-clinical aspects of the practice. In many cases, the management services they provide are more efficient and relieve the individual dentist of a great deal of non-clinical responsibility. Today, DSOs offer systems and processes as well as implementation of technology, resulting in the ability to service a wider range of patients at affordable costs. When applied properly, there is little doubt that patients can benefit.

Growth of the DSO concept expanded in earnest in the late 1990s when corporations, taking advantage of the booming stock market, started buying dental practices using their publicly traded stock instead of cash. For a while, this worked very well for the selling doctors because the stock market continued to rise. However, when the dot-com bubble burst in 2000, everyone in the stock market was impacted, and DSO share values plummeted.

Many DSOs disintegrated, either going bankrupt or giving their practices back to the selling dentists. There was substantial litigation as dentists tried to reclaim their practices or recover from their financial losses. Also, many consolidations were not profitable because broadband internet had not yet become available to small businesses, and centralized operation of practices was difficult. The majority of the DSO profit margin was in discounts on supplies and lab costs, which in the average practice only amounted to 6–7% of revenue. Even a 20% savings on those expenses would not generate enough profit to justify operating a DSO.

Gradually, DSOs restructured, technology advanced, and businesspeople with strong managerial, operational, and financial skills began to refine and expand the services to the point where there was significant profit, along with tangible benefits for the selling dentists.

The marketplace has drastically changed in the last few decades. Dentists typically graduate with a substantial amount of student loan debt, making it much more difficult to own a dental practice. It costs significantly more to set up and equip a dental practice than it did thirty years ago. A declining number of new graduates are interested in owning their own dental practices. This makes the DSO model very attractive to young dentists.

The complexity of providing a range of consolidated services without being directly involved with providing clinical services is what makes a DSO so different from a typical corporate franchise model (e.g., a fast-food chain). In a franchise model, the franchisor has complete control and dictates everything that the franchisee does, from the clothes that employees wear to the words that are spoken when a customer enters the door. That level of oversight is not permissible with a DSO due to regulatory restrictions and could never work in a service-type business where each patient has unique needs. DSOs are barred from crossing the line between outside management to inside clinical decision-making and can be subject to federal, state, and local scrutiny, both criminal and civil, if such "lines" are crossed. Such heightened levels of legal scrutiny make forming and operating a DSO a legal minefield that should only be carefully navigated with the help of experienced professionals.

Each state has a different definition of what it means to "practice dentistry." For example, in some states, the definition of practicing dentistry includes the ownership of the dental equipment, which means that in those states, the DSO is barred from owning such clinical assets. Such regulations, however, are sometimes very nuanced (and sometimes rather Byzantine). The goal of state regulators is to protect the profession of dentistry, although sometimes with a heavy regulatory hand or an archaic view of the profession.

There are now billions of dollars of investment money flowing through the DSO market. The reason DSOs attract so much capital is because of the potential profitability of the dental business model. As a business, a dental practice is unique because it typically has a much higher ratio of fixed expenses to variable expenses than most other businesses. When you can implement economies of scale and maximize the utilization of fixed overhead, you capture greater profit. This is particularly true if you can grow the practice through increased top-line revenue since a significant portion of that revenue will fall to the bottom line as profit.

Heartland Dental, currently the largest DSO in the country, adds an average of 100 new practices a year, with a healthy mixture of both start-up practices and acquisitions. Although many DSOs use the acquisition model, others (e.g., Pacific Dental and Aspen Dental) primarily build what is referred to as *de novo* practices (or "start-ups"). These are practices built from the ground up with no initial patient base. Dentists are then hired as associates to work at the facility.

There is now considerable activity with smaller DSOs being acquired by larger DSOs. Some individuals have done this multiple times, building up a group of practices and selling them at a substantial profit and then doing it all over again. Of course, the reason for such repeat activity is that a dental practice, when operating at peak efficiency, can be extremely profitable.

All DSOs are different. They have different cultures and different levels of control. Some are backed by large financial institutions, while others are funded by bank debt, existing cash flow, or private investors. Some operate under a single brand name, and others operate invisibly behind the scenes, retaining the existing brand of each practice acquired. Some are run by business executives who have come from outside the dental industry, while others are run by groups of dentists who band together. It is a sophisticated business model, and it is evolving all the time.

HOW DSOS MAKE MONEY

DSOs are in the business of providing management and support services to dental practices and charging a management fee for those services. They operate on the theory that they can do two things: manage the practice more efficiently, and therefore more profitably, and use their business IQ to increase the revenue of the practice with systems, processes, technology, and marketing. In other words, DSOs seek to provide equal or better service for less money, use negotiating power to receive better fees, and add new patients to the practice. It is simple math.

As discussed earlier, a dental practice is a unique business model where the profitability increases significantly once the fixed overhead costs are met. Dental offices tend to have support staff who are responsible for multiple tasks throughout the day. By assigning a single person or group to each specific task, and by utilizing the talents of highly-skilled professionals in finance, operations, marketing and other areas, DSOs are able to function at optimum efficiency. In addition, by negotiating higher insurance reimbursements with carriers and discounts on equipment and consumables with suppliers, more money falls to the bottom line.

Let's look at a hypothetical dental practice both as a stand-alone business and with management by a DSO. Assume the practice is producing $1 million annually, which is made up of $700,000 in dentistry and $300,000 in hygiene. Assume further that the overhead costs are approximately 80% of the revenue, inclusive of paying the owner dentist for his work, similar to how an associate would be paid (in this case, $210,000). The remaining 20% ($200,000) would be paid to the owner as a profit distribution. Therefore, of the $1 million in revenue, at the end of the year, the owner would take home $410,000.

Now let's assume the dentist sells the practice and a DSO takes over the management. The dentist remains with the practice as the sole associate and is compensated at a rate of

30% of net collections (30% of $700,000 = $210,000). This compensation rate is less than the earnings as a standalone practice because the dentist no longer owns the business and will no longer keep the profit distribution.

Two years later, however, the DSO's marketing efforts begin to pay off, and the practice is grossing $1.5 million, of which the dentist is producing $1 million and the hygiene department is producing the other $500,000. Because the former owner is producing more dentistry than before, his compensation increases to $300,000, not quite what he used to take home, but still substantial compensation with none of the managerial headaches.

Importantly, during this time, the DSO has also reduced the practice's overhead costs from 80% to 60%. This combination of reduced costs and increased production has resulted in a net profit increase from $200,000 to $600,000 (two years after the DSO took control). This is why DSOs are so attractive to both practice owners and DSO investors.

While this is, of course, an oversimplification of the process, and the legal maze that must be navigated is complex, the potential profit is the reason why owning a group of dental practices is so appealing as an investment opportunity.

The DSO staff must work to achieve this increase in profitability by providing the requisite management services. The following is a list of the various services a DSO may provide and control:

- Centralized call handling
- Insurance eligibility, processing, and billing

- Marketing strategy and services
- Clinical records management
- Payroll services
- Discounts on supplies
- Discounts on labs
- Discounts on equipment purchases
- Billing and collection services
- Information systems and tech support
- HR and personnel management
- Real estate management
- Accounting and legal services
- Financial and budget management
- Recruitment of team members and associates
- Group benefits for team members
- Ownership and management of all non-clinical assets
- Training, both clinical and non-clinical

* * *

Another benefit of consolidating dental practices is that DSOs have leverage that individual practitioners do not have. They have negotiating power with insurance companies, manufacturers and suppliers, employee benefit providers, and sometimes with landlords. DSOs are volume buyers, which often results in substantial discounts.

By way of example, when a DSO buys a practice, it has the ability to immediately approach the insurance providers of all the plans that the practice accepts and re-negotiate the reimbursement rates or, if already well established, switch the newly acquired practice to the DSO's existing fee schedule with the carriers. The DSO uses its leverage as a multi-practice owner to increase those reimbursements, often by as much as 10% or more. Because they want to maintain or expand their geographic coverage and maintain consistent quality in services for their insureds, the insurance companies are often willing to make concessions.

DSOs also have the power to negotiate substantial discounts with dental laboratories and equipment suppliers with the promise of volume-buying. Even with relatively modest effort, a DSO can increase the profitability of the practice.

This expectation of increased profitability is what allows a DSO to pay more for a practice than an individual buyer in a doctor-to-doctor transaction. Imagine that a practice is producing $1 million annually, and 70% of its revenue comes from insurance reimbursements. If a DSO acquires the practice and implements a new reimbursement schedule that is 10% higher, that $700,000 of revenue becomes $770,000. Factor in an additional $10,000 of savings on supplies and lab costs, and that practice now has $80,000 more in profits than it did before being acquired—even if collections stay flat (i.e., they do not increase).

Such savings will appear throughout the operation of the practice in the form of discounted equipment and supply purchases, group advertising, centralized insurance processing and billing, employee benefits, training programs, and the like. DSOs can put 100 dentists in a room and simultaneously improve the skills of the entire group through collaboration and training, which can positively impact the quality and efficiency of the practitioners they employ.

DSOs also possess aggregated data that help them better understand the dental consumer. They have learned that being open more days with longer hours is a consumer deliverable that is in high demand and maximizes revenue generation for a facility, given that most overhead is relatively fixed. If you use the same facility for twice as many hours a week, it is not hard to see how that maximizes utilization of fixed overhead and increases profitability. In fact, Dr. Beauchamp, the pioneer of the group practice, had Saturday office hours as early as 1940, which was unheard of at that time.

DSOs also understand that patients want high-quality dentistry that they can afford. DSOs aim their marketing and pricing toward the average consumer. They are not trying to be super high-end, fee-for-service boutiques. They offer financing, accept most quality PPO insurance plans, and will often use technology to facilitate "same-day dentistry" to decrease chair time for treatments. DSOs provide same-day dentistry for procedures that previously required a second visit, creating efficiencies that result in greater profits and a positive consumer deliverable.

It is critical to note that in no situation should a DSO tell participating dentists how to treat patients. The dentist works for the practice, which is owned by the "friendly dentist." (See section on DSO Limitations below.)

The third way that DSOs profit, of course, is if they sell or recapitalize their company. The goal of a DSO is often to build a valuable asset that continues to yield more and more profit every year; at some point, however, the DSO is likely to be sold or recapitalized. Profitable DSOs, especially growing ones, will sell for prices that are materially greater than the prices paid by the DSO to acquire the practices in their portfolio. By consolidating practices and aggregating greater earnings, the value of the enterprise increases, often resulting in significant liquidity events for the DSO.

CHAPTER TWO

Four Ways to Affiliate with a DSO

Most DSO transactions require two separate corporate entities: a management company and a professional entity. The professional entity is typically owned by either the selling dentist or a "friendly dentist" who often has a significant interest in the success of the DSO (e.g., through an equity stake in the DSO).

Although we refer to a DSO as "buying a practice" throughout this book for the sake of simplicity, in actuality, there are two transactions that happen concurrently. One is the purchase of the non-clinical assets of the practice by the DSO entity (i.e., physical assets, intellectual property, certain contracts, and goodwill). The other is the purchase of the clinical assets by the professional entity such as patient records, "contract privity" with the insurance carriers, employment of the licensed clinicians (i.e., licensed dentists and, if appropriate, hygienists), and whatever else the state where the practice is located requires to be owned by a professional entity.

The DSO is the operational and management entity. As the management arm of the practice, the DSO is responsible for all aspects of running the practice other than the actual treatment of patients and related clinical decisions. The professional entity, on the other hand, is responsible for providing the dental services. The practice collects money from the patients and pays a management fee to the DSO in exchange for its management services. In most cases, after paying the salaries of the clinical staff, nearly 100% of the remaining practice revenue will be paid to the DSO. The payment of management fees to a DSO is regulated under both state and federal laws, and this structure is highly scrutinized through regulatory oversight. There are legal limitations that prohibit DSOs from extracting all of the remaining profits from the practice. Nevertheless, experience dictates that nearly all DSOs ignore these legal limitations.

Consolidation of healthcare providers is not a new concept. It is so prevalent on the medical side that today only a small percentage of physicians are completely independent. The cost of medical equipment and supplies, the challenges of staffing, the cost and infrastructure to comply with best practices, regulatory compliance and insurance copay requirements, and the benefits of integrating many specialists into a single facility have made consolidation a practical and profitable option for most private practitioners.

There are four primary ways for a dentist to affiliate with a DSO. These are listed below then illustrated with an example of each.

1. Selling all or a portion of the practice to a DSO
2. Partnering with a DSO
3. Creating your own dentist-owned DSO
4. Working as an associate for a DSO

EXAMPLE 1: THE SELLER DENTIST

Dr. Steven Sellers is ten years from retirement. His daughter, who went to dental school and who he hoped would take over his practice, has married another dentist and moved 2,000 miles away. A few dentists in his area have offered to buy his practice, but the offers have not been appealing, and he is not ready to stop practicing. He also knows he needs to add new technology, but he is reluctant to make such a large investment this close to his retirement.

A DSO approaches Dr. Sellers and offers to buy his practice. The DSO gives him the option of retaining 20% of his ownership and requires that he work for at least five years after the closing of the transaction. The purchase price is higher than any prior offer. The opportunity to retain ownership excites Dr.

Sellers because he believes that the practice will be even more valuable over time with the assistance of the DSO.

He brings in his legal team, negotiates the terms, and makes the deal.

EXAMPLE 2: THE PARTNER DENTIST

Dr. Patricia Paterson considers herself an entrepreneur. Since graduating from dental school, she has started her own practice and has purchased three more. She was able to do this through a series of bank loans, but now that her debt-to-income ratio is higher, those banks are refusing to lend her more money. She sees great opportunities in the marketplace, but despite her continued success with each practice, she has hit a roadblock due to a lack of additional funding. It is also becoming clear that she needs an experienced executive team to manage her growing enterprise.

Dr. Paterson begins searching for outside investors or a financial partner and eventually receives an offer from a DSO that is looking to establish a footprint in her market.

The DSO presents her with a letter of intent that outlines a proposed partnership whereby the DSO will acquire a 60% ownership interest in each of her practices and provide a well-established management team to assist with administrative support and growth opportunities. Dr. Paterson will retain a 40% ownership interest in her practices; she will remain the CEO and will even have the opportunity to purchase a small equity interest in the larger DSO enterprise if she chooses to do so. Most importantly, given her successful track record, the DSO wants Dr. Paterson to continue to identify and acquire new practices and help expand the brand within her geographic region.

She brings in her legal team, negotiates the terms, and makes the deal.

EXAMPLE 3: THE INDEPENDENT DENTIST

After graduating from dental school, Dr. Isabelle Ivy moved across the country and acquired four practices, just like her twin sister, Patricia Paterson. The sisters both share the same entrepreneurial spirit, but unlike Dr. Paterson, Dr. Ivy is not willing to "sell out" to a DSO. Instead, she is determined to beat the DSOs at their own game, or at least understand the DSO model and borrow a few strategies from their playbook.

Unfortunately, like her sister, Dr. Ivy has hit a roadblock with financing because she is over-leveraged, and she reaches out to her attorney to discuss other methods for expansion. After a very successful strategy session, Dr. Ivy leaves her attorney's office with a plan to create her own DSO.

First, with the help of her legal team, she will create her own management company. Second, she will offer the key associates in each of her practice locations the opportunity to purchase a minority interest and have real equity ownership in the practice where they work. Third, she will identify doctors approaching retirement age as well as struggling offices in and around her community that may be interested in selling. Fourth, she will make offers to these practice owners by proposing a purchase price that does not require bank financing. Instead, she will pay an "earn-out" over a five-year term from the future profits of that location. Finally, her legal team will create management services agreements between her new management company (her personal DSO) and each of her practice locations that will outline the services her DSO will provide and the fee each practice will pay.

Dr. Ivy is very excited about this plan because it will allow her to continue acquiring practices and cut back her clinical hours to one day per week, enabling her to focus on being a "CEO Dentist."

Dr. Ivy is also hoping that when other dentists learn about her DSO and its ability to provide superior services for less money, they may hire her to help manage their practices and benefit from her economies of scale and centralized overhead.

EXAMPLE 4: THE ASSOCIATE DENTIST

Dr. Adam Aspen just graduated from Loma Linda School of Dentistry and has $420,000 of student loan debt. He was considered one of the top students in his class and has approached a number of practices in search of a full-time associate position. Unfortunately, the salaries they are offering mean that he will be struggling to pay off his loans for at least twenty years, and many of them do not even have the technology Dr. Aspen was using in dental school.

Dr. Aspen has no interest in ever owning a practice. He looks forward to settling down and starting a family, and the additional stress of running a business does not appeal to him at all. Working as an associate, performing great dentistry, and making a nice living are Dr. Aspen's ideal goals.

He is then recruited by a DSO-managed, multi-specialty practice. The offer is very appealing for a number of reasons. First, the salary is substantially higher than any other offer. Second, the benefits package has everything Dr. Aspen could have hoped for, including health insurance, 401K, malpractice insurance, cell phone allowance, licensing fees, continuing education reimbursement, and loan repayment assistance.

After reviewing the offer with his attorney, Dr. Aspen has a clear understanding of what is expected of him and the limitations and risks associated with the offer. The only downside to the deal is that, upon termination of his employment, Dr. Aspen will be barred from working at any other dental office within a twenty-mile radius of the practice. He ultimately decides that he is comfortable with this arrangement and signs the associate employment agreement.

* * *

If you are looking to sell to a DSO, partner with a DSO, or work for a DSO, this book is for you. Our goal is to answer all of your questions and provide you with some of our personal insight and experience along the way. If, on the other hand, you are hoping to maintain the private ownership of your practice and beat DSOs at their own game, check out chapters 8 and 9.

CHAPTER THREE

The Pros and Cons of Selling to (or Partnering with) a DSO

As with anything, there are both risks and rewards to selling a practice to a DSO. However, to understand the pros and cons of selling a practice, one must first understand how DSOs are organized and how transactions are structured.

DSO TRANSACTION STRUCTURE

The basic corporate structure of a DSO is fairly standard. Nearly every DSO is comprised of a group of investors that form a corporate entity, known as the "holding company." That holding company then forms a wholly-owned subsidiary to act as the management company or "DSO." The investors, which may or may not include private equity or venture capital firms, provide the money to acquire practices and set up the management services operation. In some cases, the holding company will also form a separate real estate entity to hold the leases for all practices under management. (See Diagram 1.)

DIAGRAM 1

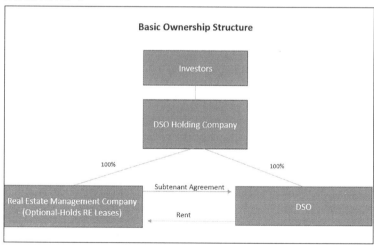

When a DSO wants to acquire a practice, it must decide two things. First, will the DSO acquire the non-clinical assets directly, or will it create a subsidiary (known as a "sub-DSO") to acquire the non-clinical assets? Second, the DSO must decide who will own the practice entity that will take custody of the patient records and acquire the other clinical assets. If the DSO has a "friendly dentist" in the state where the practice is located, the friendly dentist will form a new practice entity to purchase the clinical assets. If the DSO does not have a friendly dentist in that particular state, it will likely ask the selling dentist to remain as the owner of the clinical assets or to become the owner of the professional entity that acquires the clinical assets. In either event, the DSO or sub-DSO will enter into a "management services agreement" with the practice entity.

Due to this bifurcation of the clinical and non-clinical assets, DSO acquisitions typically involve two simultaneous transactions: a sale of the non-clinical assets to the DSO and a sale of the clinical assets to a professional entity owned by a licensed dentist.

The professional entity serves a primary purpose: to legally control the ownership of the practice and its patient list and records. Money flows into the professional practice from patients and insurance companies for professional dental services rendered and then out to the DSO in the form of a management fee.

Where the DSO does not use sub-DSOs but instead offers rollover equity as part of the consideration, the selling dentist gets a minority interest in the entire enterprise (i.e., the master DSO), which includes all practices under management. (See Diagram 2.)

DIAGRAM 2

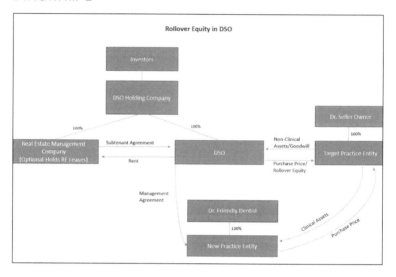

Alternatively, when a DSO uses sub-DSOs to acquire the non-clinical assets, and the purchase price includes rollover equity, that equity is typically offered in the sub-DSO. This means that the selling dentist is essentially retaining equity in his or her own practice because the sub-DSO will only generate revenue from that particular practice. (See Diagram 3.)

DIAGRAM 3

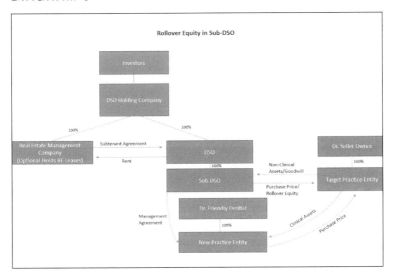

The purchase price structure in a dental practice acquisition varies by DSO but will contain some or all of the following elements:

- **Cash Payment:** Cash paid to the seller on the closing date.
- **Rollover Equity:** Ownership interest offered to the selling dentist in either the DSO or sub-DSO and, in some cases, a combination of both.
- **Indemnification Escrow:** A fixed dollar amount (usually 5–10% of the purchase price) that is held in escrow for a fixed period of time (usually 12–24 months) to cover any indemnification claims that may arise during that period. In the event that the DSO experiences a financial loss as a result of the seller's

operation of the practice prior to the closing, or because of a seller breach of the purchase agreement, the DSO can recoup its losses from the indemnification escrow. Any money remaining in escrow at the end of the holding period is released to the seller.

- **Holdback:** A fixed dollar amount that is held in reserve to ensure that the practice generates a certain amount of revenue during a particular period after the closing date. Once the holding period expires, the money will be released to the seller or the DSO, depending on whether the practice exceeds the target revenue threshold.

- **Earn-out:** A portion of the sale price that is directly dependent upon the future success of the practice. For example, a DSO may want to incentivize the seller to continue growing the practice after the closing but may not want to offer additional rollover equity. In that case, the DSO may offer to pay the seller an "earn-out bonus" based on future earnings.

DSOs mix and match these elements based on their own corporate approach and philosophy.

PURCHASE PRICE

The first potential advantage to selling to a DSO, and what appeals most to dentists, is that DSOs almost always offer to pay more for a practice than an individual, private practitioner buyer. For decades, the rule of thumb when valuing practices was to multiply the practice's annual gross collections by approximately 60% to 80%, depending on the type and quality of practice. DSOs typically value practices based on a multiple of EBITDA (described below), which can often equate to anywhere from 100% to 200% of gross collections.

Generally speaking, DSOs are backed by sophisticated investors who analyze a dental practice's profit potential and return on investment if operated with greater efficiency as part of a consolidated group rather than solely based on revenue potential. This is why so much investment money is pouring into the dental industry. Consolidated group practices can be very profitable entities. For this reason, the financial analysis of a practice's value is typically based on a metric known as EBITDA.

EBITDA is an accounting term that stands for "earnings before interest, taxes, depreciation, and amortization." Think of it as a "pure" measure of a business's profitability. The practice's various expenses certainly affect its cash flow as well as its profitability, but EBITDA is a way of saying, "Okay, this practice generates $1 million in collections and factoring in the salaries, rents, labs, and supplies, this practice has a 62% overhead cost to produce that number."

This gives the DSO a way to compare one practice to another. The fact that one dentist has more interest expense than another or pays a different amount in taxes because of various deductions is irrelevant to the practice's profit potential as part of a multi-practice DSO.

DSOs generally base their purchase price offer on a "multiple" of EBITDA. For example, a DSO may have a model that offers a "five-times multiple" for single-location general dentistry practices and a "six-times multiple" for single-location specialty practices. To illustrate, if the DSO targets a single-location general practice producing $2 million annually and determines that the EBITDA is $500,000, it would offer a purchase price of $2.5 million ($500,000 EBITDA, multiplied by 5).

There is nothing standard about the "multiple" offered by DSOs. Even within a single DSO, its standard multiple offering may be 5X. But for a "premium" practice (i.e., perhaps one with a high-visibility location or well-respected practitioners), the DSO may offer 6X or 7X EBITDA. Large, profitable specialty practices and practices with multiple locations can potentially generate multiples as high as 9 or 10.

The DSO's first offer, as stated in a written letter of intent, is usually based on its initial financial due diligence, which includes an analysis of historical tax returns and balance sheets, typically for the past three years. Once the letter of intent is signed, the DSO will then do a much deeper dive into the practice's financials, commonly known as a "quality of earnings" or "Q of E" analysis. The Q of E is appropriately named because it is, in fact, a comprehensive analysis of the quality of the practice's earnings. This due diligence can take weeks or even months to complete. During this time, the DSO's financial and regulatory advisors will assess everything from the compensation paid to associates to provider reimbursement rates to historical accounts receivable collections. They will supply the seller with long lists of diligence requests and may even audit patient records.

In many cases, the Q of E will uncover various "one-offs" and "add-backs" that negatively impact the seller's bottom line and result in a lower EBITDA. This includes extraneous deductions or expenses that the DSO does not intend to finance after closing. Examples include personal cars and vacations paid for by the practice, salaries of family members, and the like. These benefits will disappear after the closing.

The DSO will also "normalize" some of the numbers as it makes its EBITDA calculation. For example, many practice owners do not pay themselves a fixed salary but instead, take whatever money is left after all expenses are paid. In this case, the DSO may insert a number into its calculation that it expects to pay the seller (or another associate) to produce the same level of dentistry. Such normalization is important to understand. Many dentists will do a quick calculation of their profit, including everything they take home, and expect to receive a multiple of that number. That is not how it works. The DSO assumes that you will be working for the practice after the sale and will be getting paid 30–40% of your collections. They will then reduce your EBITDA by that amount. Once the quality of earnings analysis is complete, the DSO will inform the seller of the "actual EBITDA" based on that analysis. Once the actual EBITDA is finalized, the multiple is then re-applied to calculate the updated purchase price.

To illustrate, assume you operate a $2 million practice with 60% overhead. You currently take home $800,000; if the DSO is offering a 5X multiple, you might assume that the value of your practice is $4 million. But think again. The DSO is going to deduct what they must pay you as an associate; let's say, $300,000. This reduces the DSO's anticipated profit to $500,000 and, in turn, reduces the value of your practice to $2.5 million. It's a big difference.

Thus far, we have focused on how DSOs value a practice as a whole. Determining the valuation is only the first step in the process; how payment of that valuation is structured is equally important. Many DSOs are simply not willing to pay 100% of the value of the practice in cash at closing. Instead, many DSOs prefer to purchase a majority share of the practice (typically anywhere from 60% to 90%), with the seller retaining a minority ownership interest in the practice. As a minority partner, the seller will share in the profits of the practice but will likely have no voting rights and no real decision-making authority with respect to non-clinical matters. In addition, liquidating that minority ownership may be difficult or impossible until the DSO itself is sold or recapitalized.

If a dentist believes the practice is going to grow or will become more valuable after the sale, then retaining partial ownership is an advantage, especially if the DSO is paying a much higher purchase price than the historical valuation model. For example, if you have a partial fee-for-service and PPO practice collecting $2 million annually, with a robust patient base in a modern facility, you may get $1.6 million in a private sale (based on the formula of 80% x 1 year of gross collections). A DSO, on the other hand, may value your practice at $3 million but only be willing to acquire 80% of the practice. Upon closing, you may receive a purchase price of $1.6 million, which is the same price you would have received in a private sale, but you still retain 20% ownership going forward. Upon a future sale of the DSO, you will be entitled to a second payday in exchange for your retained 20% interest.

MANAGEMENT RESPONSIBILITIES

The other obvious advantage to selling to a DSO is not having the headache and responsibility of running the practice. After the closing, in theory, you will be able to focus all your time and energy on practicing dentistry, improving your skills, and giving your patients the best care. You no longer need to worry about HR issues, payroll, insurance carriers, collections, or any other operational aspects of the practice. For some dentists, this is very appealing. Some do not feel they are particularly adept at management and simply want to treat patients. Sometimes dentists get burned out and tired of running their practices.

All DSOs are different. Some will leave considerable operational control with you. Some will give you total control. Others will take over every aspect of the practice, other than clinical decisions and actual treatment. Some tell you which laboratories you can use and whom you can buy supplies from, while others do not. Prior to closing, it is important to understand all the requirements and restrictions that will come with the acquisition by and affiliation with the DSO.

For legal reasons, a DSO will not tell you how to treat patients. But you may feel some pressure to produce or push more expensive procedures. Remember, DSOs are in business to maximize and extract profit. They have investors looking for a substantial return. It is a very different dynamic than a dentist owning his or her practice.

FUTURE INCOME

There are two potential disadvantages that may occur when selling to a DSO. First, the selling dentist may experience a decrease in monthly income. This is typically because the seller previously had been enjoying the benefits of being the business owner (i.e., taking all the practice's profits). After the closing, the seller is only paid for his personal production (ranging anywhere from 30–40%, commonly averaging around 33–35%, of personal collections).

The second disadvantage when selling to a DSO also relates to income. As part of a sale of the business, the seller will lose the economic advantages of owning a business. The seller may have been writing off certain business expenses or enjoyed "working vacations" every year by combining continuing education with a trip to Hawaii or the Bahamas.

Many dentists are able to write off a variety of expenses through their practices. Of course, that stops when a DSO takes over. This represents a potential material loss in income because even if a seller is being paid the same amount as he or she had earned before the sale, that seller now would be paying for those expenses personally. The change from business owner to employee needs to be factored into any evaluation of the deal. Most dental accountants can run a *pro forma* to determine what a seller's net income will look like after a sale and how that compares to the pre-closing income. This is a very important step in the seller's due diligence process.

FUTURE EMPLOYMENT

Another big differentiator between private sales and DSO sales is the post-closing employment requirement. In almost every case, a DSO buyer will require that the seller dentist continue to work at the practice for a minimum of three to five years. DSOs would not be able to acquire practices at their current pace if they had to find new practitioners with each acquisition. Instead, they rely heavily on the commitment of the seller doctor to continue treating patients after closing.

Private buyers, on the other hand, may not want the seller doctor to stick around for quite as long. For example, a purchasing doctor will often need to service significant debt in order to make the purchase and, in such cases, will need to produce most of the revenue, as opposed to paying someone else to do so. This obviously depends on the specific circumstances of the transaction, but if you are a doctor looking to retire at the time of the sale or shortly after closing, you will likely need to find a private buyer.

ROLLOVER EQUITY

As discussed in detail earlier in this chapter, rollover equity comes in two forms: ownership in the master DSO or ownership in a sub-DSO that only holds your practice's non-clinical assets. A sub-DSO isolates the practice as its sole asset within the master DSO. In some limited cases, there could be a combination of the two.

Rollover equity is a benefit offered by some but not all DSOs. The inclusion of rollover equity in an offer can be attractive for a number of reasons. First, if you are in a position like Dr. Paterson (chapter 2's "Partner Dentist") and you have started expanding to multiple facilities and need the capital to support your growth, affiliating with a DSO may make a lot of sense. But, keep in mind, you will no longer be calling the shots. Even if you are still the CEO and retaining certain day-to-day authority, you will be a minority owner, with most major decisions being controlled by the majority owner DSO.

Second, rollover equity means that you are still an equity owner of a business. As such, you may receive distributions from the business that help supplement your income. The specifics surrounding these distribution rights will be set forth in an agreement governing the relationship between the owners (known as a "Shareholders' Agreement" when the entity is a corporation, an "Operating Agreement" when the entity is an LLC, or a "Partnership Agreement" when the business is operated as a partnership). For convenience, we will be using the term "Partnership Agreement" to refer to any agreement between the owners.

Third, in most cases, you will not be required to pay tax on the value of the rollover equity at the time of the sale. Typically, the transaction can be structured so that the rollover equity is issued to the seller in exchange for a contribution (rather than a sale) of a portion of the practice's assets. Thanks to Section 351 of the Internal Revenue Code, this means that there will be no tax on the value of the rollover equity until it is later sold.

The fourth benefit of rollover equity is the opportunity to sell that equity at a higher value in the future. Keep in mind that you are an investor in the business, just like the other DSO investors, and they are waiting for the opportunity to sell the DSO at a higher multiple. You already sold the practice once, but when the DSO investors are ready to cash out, you will get a second payday for the rollover equity you are holding.

There are many positive aspects that come with receiving rollover equity, but it is equally important to understand the risks involved. Such risks will be outlined in detail in the Partnership Agreement. A good dental attorney, experienced in these types of transactions, will do a thorough analysis of the Partnership Agreement and present you with a detailed memo or explanation outlining the risks, as well as the rights, involved with your investment. The following is a brief overview of some of the risks and restrictions that may be attached to your rollover equity:

- **Transfer Restrictions.** You will likely have no ability to sell, transfer, or encumber your equity until the DSO experiences a sale or recapitalization or perhaps when you retire permanently from practicing. This means you are holding a relatively illiquid investment.

- **Drag-along Rights.** In the event the majority owner(s) decides to sell the company, you will have no choice but to sell your interest upon the terms and purchase price dictated by the majority owner(s). You will (figuratively) be "dragged along" in such a sale.

- **Dilution.** The majority owner(s) may have the option to (and most likely will) issue additional equity in the company from time to time, which will dilute your interest in the business. During the negotiation phase, experienced counsel can usually negotiate some anti-dilution provisions that give you the option to make matching capital contributions to avoid being diluted.

- **No "Put Option."** A put option is the right of an equity holder to require the company to buy back some or all of his or her equity in the company. In our experience, it is rare for a partnership agreement to initially grant the seller dentist a right to cash out of the DSO. In many cases, we have been successful in advocating for our seller clients to obtain a separate agreement that allowed them to cash out some or all of their equity after the passage of some time.

- **No Voting Rights.** It is highly unlikely that a minority partner will have any real management or voting rights. In some cases, the selling dentist is offered limited voting rights or even a seat on a board, allowing the doctor to at least have a "voice," but even in those cases, he or she can be outvoted by the majority partners.

One of the biggest differences between getting equity in the master DSO versus a sub-DSO is what happens upon a liquidity event. Let us illustrate how this plays out in both scenarios.

Master DSO: Dr. Fung sold his practice to HappyDocs for $1 million. The purchase price was based on his EBITDA of $200,000, multiplied by five. He received $700,000 in cash at closing and rollover equity in HappyDocs valued at $300,000. HappyDocs is the master DSO and its value at the time of Dr. Fung's acquisition was $300 million. So, Dr. Fung is the owner of 0.1% of HappyDocs. For the next four years, Dr. Fung shows up for work, does his job, and the practice's revenue stays pretty consistent.

After four years, HappyDocs is sold and the net proceeds of the sale are $900 million. Dr. Fung receives $900,000 in exchange for his 0.1% interest. This means he effectively sold his $1 million practice for $1.6 million ($700,000 on the first sale, *plus* $900,000 on the second sale).

Now, let's look at a second example involving rollover equity at the sub-DSO level.

Sub-DSO: Dr. Evans also sold her practice to HappyDocs for $1 million. Her purchase price was also based on a $200,000 EBITDA with a 5X multiple. However, in this case, HappyDocs created a sub-DSO to hold the non-clinical assets of Dr. Evans' practice. She received $700,000 in cash and a 30% ownership interest in the sub-DSO. For the next four years, Dr. Evans works hard to double the size of her practice. Four years later, HappyDocs sells for $900 million, of which $2M is allocated to Dr. Evans' sub-DSO. In this case, Dr. Evans will receive $600,000 in exchange for her 30% interest in the sub-DSO. Effectively, she sold her $1 million practice for $1.3 million ($700,000 on the first sale, *plus* $600,000 on the second sale).

Note that in this sub-DSO example, Dr. Evans's large payday was a direct result of the effort she contributed to growing her own practice location, while Dr. Fung basically acted as an associate and was able to collect a larger purchase price due to the overall success of the master DSO.

Now let's discuss the holdback and earn-out concepts using these same examples.

Holdback Example #1. Dr. Fung's deal includes a 10% indemnification holdback, which is held in escrow for two years. This means that $100,000 will be held in a separate escrow account to ensure the buyer's risk against future indemnification claims. During those two years, a patient sues Dr. Fung and the DSO for missed pathology that occurred prior to the closing date, and which turned out to be cancerous. The DSO's attorneys file a motion to have the claim against the DSO dismissed since it was not involved in the ownership or management of the practice at the time of treatment. The judge agrees and dismisses the claim against the DSO. The DSO spends $10,000 in legal fees to be removed from the lawsuit. That $10,000 is then released from the indemnification escrow to reimburse the DSO for its legal fees. At the end of the second year, the remaining $90,000 is released to Dr. Fung.

Earn-Out Example #1. Dr. Fung's deal also included an earn-out component, which allows Dr. Fung the opportunity to earn additional purchase price in the event he is able to increase the practice's EBITDA over the twelve months following the sale. According to the purchase agreement, on the one-year anniversary of the closing date, the buyer will calculate the trailing twelve months' EBITDA (TTM EBITDA) of the practice (i.e., the practice's EBITDA for the preceding twelve months). If TTM EBITDA has increased, Dr. Fung will be paid his 5X multiple on such increase. The buyer imposes a cap of $100,000 on the potential earn-out value. However, because Dr. Fung failed to grow the practice, his EBITDA of $200,000 remained flat, and he did not receive any additional purchase price.

Holdback Example #2. Dr. Evans had the same 10% indemnification holdback in her deal, but her attorneys negotiated for it to be released to her after one year rather than two. This does not absolve Dr. Evans of responsibility for any liabilities that relate to her practice prior to the closing, but it releases the holdback funds to her a year earlier than Dr. Fung.

Earn-Out Example #2. Dr. Evans also received the same earn-out opportunity whereby the DSO offered to pay her 5X on the TTM EBITDA growth in the year following the sale, with a cap of $100,000. Dr. Evans was excited about this opportunity because she knew she could grow the practice. Her attorneys also negotiated to remove the cap on her earn-out.

At the end of year one, Dr. Evans grew the practice's EBITDA to $240,000, resulting in an earn-out payment of $200,000 ($40,000 of TTM EBITDA growth multiplied by 5). In this scenario, Dr. Evans has received a total purchase price of $1.2 million, which is $200,000 more than the original value of her practice.

As you can see, the way that the rollover equity is structured can vary widely, and the impact on your total payout is substantial. The specific terms of how these play out can be a bit complicated, and these models are always evolving. Given the complexity of these structures, we often try to include an example or hypothetical in the letter of intent. We are now seeing deals where the selling dentist is getting equity in both the master DSO and the sub-DSO.

★ ★ ★

As always in contractual relationships, the devil is in the details. You need to have a clear understanding of how your deal is structured and understand both the potential upsides and downsides.

Keep in mind that DSOs make these deals every day. They are experts when it comes to buying practices and maximizing their profitability. On the other hand, if you are a selling dentist, this might be your only opportunity in your life to be involved in a deal like this. It is critical that you put yourself in a position to negotiate the best deal possible by surrounding yourself with the most competent team of advisors. As dental attorneys, it drives us crazy when people say that most contracts are just "boilerplate." This is not true. All of the words in contracts have meaning, and if a dispute arises, those words will be your sword or your shield.

We have all heard the success stories about the doctor who sold to private equity and made tons of money or the dentist who was able to drop down to part-time and maintain his income level after a DSO took over his practice. These are snapshots of a much larger picture. For each success story you have heard, there is another story about a doctor who lost control and wishes he had made better choices.

Do not go into a deal with blind optimism. There are law firms like ours that have handled hundreds of these transactions. There are also accounting firms with expertise in dental deals (we have worked with many) that are experienced in the twists and turns of DSO transactions. You have one chance to do this right. Make sure you surround yourself with the right team to protect yourself and maximize the value of your transaction.

There are ways to make your involvement with a DSO, or to make the creation of your own DSO, a resounding success. It is also easy to get burned if you do not fully understand the complexity of the agreements. You have the ability to negotiate beneficial terms, and our goal is to ensure a successful business transaction for everyone involved.

A DSO transaction is a serious decision, and there are many factors that need to be weighed. It is important to have a clear sense of all the pros and cons, and those will vary with each DSO you consider working with. The deal may look fantastic when you receive the initial offer letter, but the deal points can be extremely nuanced and may change when the actual deal documents are received. You may soon realize that what you are contractually committing to is vastly different than what you had expected.

CHAPTER FOUR

Preparing for Sale

I f you have spent months or years debating whether or not to sell your practice, concluding that the time is right to sell may feel like a huge relief. After reading the first three chapters of this book, you may have even decided that you would like to attract a DSO buyer. But now what? How do you find a DSO buyer? What do you need to do to prepare your practice for sale? How do you attract the highest purchase price? Where do you even begin? In this chapter, we will address all of these concerns.

FINDING A DSO BUYER

There are essentially four ways to connect with a DSO buyer:

1. Hire a practice broker.
2. Wait for the DSO to approach you.
3. Approach the DSO directly.
4. Ask someone who has relationships with DSOs for an introduction.

Let's go into detail on each one and the advantages and potential drawbacks.

Using a Practice Broker

Arguably, the easiest way to attract a DSO is to hire a dental practice broker who has experience in successfully attracting DSO buyers and closing transactions on behalf of sellers. Some brokers have long-standing relationships with DSOs and are well-positioned to "shop" your practice to every available buyer.

A good, ethical, and experienced broker can be very valuable. Typically, they will do a general assessment and valuation of your practice, give you an approximate calculation of your EBITDA, and suggest a range of offers you can expect to receive. Brokers are also great for selling dentists who want someone to guide them through the entire process, assist with negotiations, act as a middleman with the DSO and the attorneys, assist with the due diligence process, and explain the numbers.

Of course, this level of service comes at a price. Broker fees are typically based on a percentage of the purchase price, ranging anywhere from 5–10%, depending on the broker and the transaction itself. In addition, some brokers charge a non-refundable initial fee prior to preparing a valuation. In some cases, the brokers are also under contract with the DSOs, so they are collecting finders' fees from the buyer as well as the commission that you are paying as the seller.

The advantage to you as the seller is that brokers are highly incentivized to maximize your purchase price. The more money you get, the more money they get. If you decide to work with a broker, make sure you do your own due diligence on the broker. There are many people out there who claim to have the right connections with DSOs, but they really do not. If you are going to get your money's worth, you need to work with a broker who has real expertise in the marketplace and can give you several references from satisfied clients who have successfully closed deals with DSOs lined up by the broker.

The DSO Approaches You

DSOs are actively looking for practices to acquire. Many DSOs have merger and acquisition teams that find, negotiate, and close acquisitions. Dentists are not hard to find. Perhaps the DSO obtained your name from one of its current members or it simply did a Google search.

The advantage to you is that there are no broker fees when a DSO comes to you directly. The downside is that the DSO offer might not have arrived at the right time for you. Perhaps you are already committed to selling your practice to an associate dentist or have agreed to merge with another local practitioner.

If you are ready to sell but are not sure which way to turn, do not sit around waiting for someone to come looking for you. Get proactive.

You Approach the DSO

DSOs are not hard to find, and they are not hard to approach. As we have mentioned, they are almost always in "acquisition mode." There might even be several DSOs that are interested in your practice.

Typically, you can find the right person whom you need to speak with by visiting the DSO's website. Many of the larger DSOs attend dental conventions and have a booth you can visit to learn about their mission and culture, which could lead to a discussion about your practice. Some of the larger DSOs periodically host their own events to cultivate mutual interest.

There are at least three potential disadvantages to approaching a DSO directly. First, you now appear to be a motivated seller. Second, you might know very little about the DSO except what it tells you or what it has pumped into the marketplace through its own public relations (unless you have done your homework, which you should). Third, without a third party advocating on your behalf, you may miss out on an opportunity to negotiate optimum deal terms.

In our experience, approaching a DSO does not necessarily put a potential seller at a disadvantage. Large DSOs are operated by sophisticated businesspeople who are not in the habit of playing games. Whether you find the DSO through a broker or whether the DSO approaches you or you approach it, the DSO "intake" process tends to remain consistent and, for the most part, fair.

Request an Introduction

Law and accounting firms that specialize in representing dentists handle transactions with DSOs regularly. Our own firm has relationships with dozens of DSOs, and very often, they will ask us if any of our clients are interested in selling. Because of our experience and familiarity with the DSO marketplace, we are in a unique position to advise our clients as to which DSOs may be the best fit for their particular practice and sometimes to make a critical introduction.

There are multiple advantages to this "introduction" approach. First, since we have a history with these DSOs, they know we have hundreds of dental clients, some of whom may want to consider selling their practices. The DSOs clearly want to maintain a positive relationship with us. Second, as your counsel and your referral source to the DSOs, we may be familiar with your particular practice and understand which DSOs might be the right fit. Third, based on our experience and prior transactions, we may have intimate knowledge of the "hot button" issues of each DSO.

At our firm, it is not uncommon for us to represent multiple sellers transacting with a particular DSO at the same time. We are familiar with the deal terms and exactly what can and cannot be negotiated. We also have the experience of knowing if your multiple of EBITDA is fair or if it is "below market" compared to all the other deals we are handling.

In short, this is likely the largest dental transaction you will close in your lifetime. Take your time, ask for help, and make sure you understand every aspect of the deal before you sign anything (even a non-binding letter of intent). Do not put your signature on any document without prior review by your lawyer and your accountant.

HOW TO PREPARE FOR A SALE

If you are thinking about selling your practice to a DSO, whether it is this year or in the next two or three years, we recommend that you take certain steps to prepare your practice for sale.

Understand that when a DSO acquires you, it will conduct extensive due diligence on your practice. It will review your tax returns, financial statements, insurance policies, employment contracts, vendor agreements, provider agreements, accounts receivable history, your mix of payors, collections by provider, patient complaints, IT and data protection policies, employee benefits, real estate leases, and much, much more. You will be bombarded with lengthy due diligence request lists, not only from the DSO's internal analysts but also from its law firm, its accounting firm, its regulatory experts, its insurance advisors, and the like. This is a level of scrutiny and business sophistication you have likely not previously endured.

The best way to prepare for this thorough investigation is to conduct your own due diligence ahead of time. By conducting your own internal examination of your practice, you can eliminate or at least reduce the risk of any surprises that could potentially blow up your deal or reduce your purchase price. This also gives you ample time to make any necessary corrections or adjustments. We refer to this pre-sale, self-imposed due diligence as "sell-side diligence." Examples of due diligence that you can complete prior to a sale include:

- **Running lien searches on the practice.** This is the best way to find out what debts will need to be paid off at closing. You may also find old liens on the practice that have not been terminated. Sometimes getting these liens removed can take weeks and have been known to delay a closing. You may also uncover unknown judgments of record or tax liens you did not know existed or that were resolved but never removed from the public record.

- **Financial due diligence.** Ask your accountant to review your financials to determine what items will result in potential pitfalls when determining your EBITDA calculation.

- **Associate classification.** Consult with your attorneys to make sure all associates are properly classified as employees or independent contractors. The DSO is going to examine all staff members in the practice to determine if they are properly classified. If the classification is improper, they will make an adjustment in their projections based on the expense of that employee going forward. Misclassification could have a negative impact on your EBITDA or multiple, not to mention that it may cause problems with both state and federal regulatory agencies.

- **Running searches on key personnel.** DSOs typically run Google and social media searches not only on you but on all key personnel. It is important that you know what is out there before they do. We had a dentist client who, years ago, had a "legal complication" in her life. We knew this doctor to be a good person of high integrity, but she made a mistake. In the end, she was able to get her record expunged, but when the DSO conducted a Google search on her, a single newspaper article appeared detailing her arrest. This reflected very unfavorably on her because she thought the expungement had cleared the issue, but she was unaware of an old article buried three pages down on Google. At the time, she had multiple offers from DSOs. Some of them walked away from their offers, not because of the incident but because she failed to disclose it to them.

- **Restrictive covenants.** One of the biggest mistakes we see with selling doctors is their failure to enter into thorough, written employment agreements with associate dentists. DSOs want to know that if an associate dentist refuses to stay with the practice after the sale, that associate will be barred from soliciting the patients, referral sources, and staff of the practice and from opening a competing practice within the surrounding area. If you are preparing for a sale and do not have written agreements in place with associate dentists, take the time to address this deficiency, making sure there are restrictive covenants in place and that the covenants are freely assignable by you, as the employer, in the event of a sale of the practice.

Bear in mind that anything that occurs before the sale of your practice is *your* responsibility. You will be indemnifying the DSO against all liabilities relating to the practice prior to the closing date. For example, if prior to closing you paid your office manager as an "exempt" salaried employee with no eligibility for overtime and the DSO determines (based on applicable law) that your office manager should have been paid as a "non-exempt" hourly employee, then after the transaction closes that employee will be reclassified as an hourly employee. The office manager may then claim an entitlement to overtime for her past years working for you. Such overtime liability will fall on you, not the DSO, because it relates to the practice prior to the closing.

Any "clean-up" matters that involve the associates and staff members (e.g., unused vacation days, expense reimbursements) should be resolved prior to the sale. Failure to do so may have negative implications for your deal. After a buyer enters the picture, the employees may realize that they have some leverage and might start making unreasonable demands. We had a client who lost his buyer because his associate, who was by far the largest producer for the practice, refused to sign a non-compete. On another occasion, we represented the seller of a specialty practice in an eight-figure transaction, and the associate refused to sign the buyer's form of employment agreement unless the seller paid him $1 million. In another transaction, our seller client had an associate with no written employment agreement but had worked for the practice for fourteen years. As the closing approached, the associate told the seller that he would only commit to staying with the practice after the sale if he received equity in the DSO at closing.

Do your homework in advance. Button up your practice before you go to market. Doing so will make the process a lot less stressful, and you will eliminate (or reduce the chance of) surprises. Clean up any messes and put yourself in the best possible position to negotiate a great deal that will lead you to a successful outcome.

* * *

CHOOSING THE RIGHT DSO

If you take the time to prepare your practice for sale, you may position yourself to receive multiple DSO offers, which happens more often than people realize. If you find yourself in this enviable position, you will need to be prepared to choose between the various DSOs.

As we have mentioned several times throughout this book, DSOs come in many different forms. The distinguishing factors include, but are not limited to:

- The size and geographic footprint of the organization;
- Rollover equity opportunities and the likelihood of a second liquidity event;
- Length of employment requirements;
- Historical track record and reputation;
- Purchase price (i.e., multiple of EBITDA) being offered;
- DSO-branded practices vs. individually-branded practices;
- Control philosophy;
- Type of practices targeted (general, specialty, or mixed);
- Corporate culture;
- Management philosophy;

- Long-term and short-term business plans;
- Capital backing;
- Amount of debt leverage; and
- Expectations of you as a seller and "employee."

If you receive multiple DSO offers, the first thing you will do is compare the terms of the offer letters. This should be done with the assistance of your attorneys and accountants. Keep in mind that the offer with the highest purchase price may not actually be the best offer. The fine print may include holdbacks, escrows, and other contingencies or future performance requirements that make the overall offer less appealing.

The next thing we recommend is that you ask for references. It is always a good idea to talk to other dentists who have sold their practice to the DSO you are considering. You are about to enter into what may very well be a life-changing business transaction. Take your time and gather all the facts. One important benefit to working with attorneys and accountants who specialize in DSO transactions is that they are able to advise you on which DSOs have the best track records and which ones make the best partners. They will also be able to share the post-closing experiences of their clients who have already transacted with the DSO.

Do your homework! This is the time to ask all of your questions. Do not be afraid of scaring off a potential buyer. These are hard-core, sophisticated businesspeople who are not easily offended, and they are "all business all the time." The following is a list of questions that we recommend asking before signing a letter of intent:

1. Can you provide me with the names of three other doctors who have been acquired by your DSO?
2. What benefits do you offer your doctors?
3. Will my associates be asked to sign new employment agreements?
4. Do you plan to retain all of my staff, and will their salaries and benefits remain the same?
5. How involved will you be in the day-to-day management of the office (and how involved will I remain)?
6. Will the name of the practice be changed?
7. Will I be restricted to ordering supplies from certain vendors and only using specified labs?
8. Will you maintain the current office hours?
9. Will my work schedule change?
10. Are you planning to change the practice management software?
11. Will you continue to accept the same insurance providers (and will I be required to participate with new insurance providers you add)?
12. Are you backed by a private equity firm? If so, what is the name of the firm, and when did they acquire an ownership interest in the DSO? How much capital have they made available for continued investment?
13. What is your current EBITDA?
14. What is the goal or business plan to achieve your next liquidity event (sale or recapitalization)?
15. How do my practice and location fit into your overall business plan?

16. How many practices do you have under management?
17. In what states do you currently operate, and do you have plans to expand into different markets?
18. Do you offer rollover equity? If so, is the equity in the master DSO or in a sub-DSO?
19. How much vacation will I be permitted to take?
20. Do you intend to continue at my location long-term?
21. What percentage of your doctors achieve their earn-out or receive their holdbacks? Can I speak to some who have?
22. Can you show me your internal spreadsheets and assumptions on how you arrived at my EBITDA calculation?

It is also important to note that not every DSO is successful. Some have been around for decades and have a well-established track record. Each year more and more DSOs enter the marketplace, but not all are successful.

Several years ago, we represented a doctor who sold his practice to a DSO and continued working at the office as an associate. The DSO did very little to reduce expenses and did even less to grow the practice. As a result, profits remained flat. The DSO was acquiring practices at an alarming rate, paying top dollar, but failed to invest adequate time and energy in perfecting the back-office infrastructure or to develop the brand and business plan. In other words, it was not capitalizing on many of the things needed for success. Instead, the DSO was singularly focused on adding new locations to its portfolio.

We were not at all surprised when the selling doctor called to inform us that the DSO's private equity firm had frozen any future acquisitions and ultimately decided to liquidate. As a result, the DSO had to sell off the lesser performing practices and even offered to sell the practice back to our client at nearly half of its original purchase price.

Certain that he could grow the business, our client bought his practice back from the DSO in a "fire sale." Thereafter, our firm matched the client with a small but well-run DSO that agreed to buy the practice from our client dentist for the original sale price. In the end, our fortunate client managed to sell the same practice twice for the sale purchase price, leaving him with substantially more cash. This is not a typical example, of course, but it does happen, and it highlights the importance of picking the right DSO to purchase your practice.

As is true in any growing industry, sometimes over-eager investors enter the market with no understanding of the industry. Does anyone remember the dot-com bubble of the late 1990s? How about the real estate construction boom of the early 2000s?

If you are contemplating a sale of your practice to a newer DSO, be cautious. Understand its capital structure and the promises made to its investors. There are reasons why well-established DSOs protect their cash flow and develop retention structures (i.e., rollover equity, holdbacks, and earnouts) to keep the selling doctors active and engaged in the continued success of the practice.

CHAPTER FIVE

Understanding the Transaction Process

PHASE 1: OFFER/LETTER OF INTENT

Before you even get to the letter of intent ("LOI") phase, you should present your potential buyer with a non-disclosure agreement ("NDA"). If the DSO buyer gives you an NDA, be sure to have it reviewed by your counsel prior to signing it. This NDA should be executed before you provide any financial or confidential information related to the practice.

An LOI is a non-binding offer to purchase your practice. Some DSOs use very detailed LOIs, which are designed to identify most key terms of a deal. Other DSOs only include high-level deal points in the LOI. As a general rule, every LOI will include the following components:

- Practice valuation/enterprise value (i.e., estimated EBITDA and multiple);
- Purchase price;
- Percentage of the practice you will retain, if any, in the form of rollover equity;
- Payment terms, including cash paid at closing and any holdbacks, escrows, and/or earn-out terms;
- Rollover equity details (percentage, type, rights);
- Target working capital that must be left in the practice at closing;
- Post-closing employment requirements;
- Restrictive covenant terms (i.e., number of years and territory in which you are barred from practicing after closing);
- Anticipated date of closing;
- Due diligence rights;
- Closing contingencies;
- An exclusivity ("no-shop") clause;
- Confidentiality; and
- State of governing law if a dispute arises.

The letter of intent is often negotiated. Typically, the only provisions of an LOI that are binding on the parties are the "no-shop," "confidentiality," and "choice of law" clauses; however, the LOI sets the expectations of the parties. For that reason, we recommend that if you have any extraordinary requirements or important business concerns (e.g., you want the right to "put" your rollover equity after five years), they should be negotiated into the LOI.

Every LOI will include certain contingencies that must be satisfied in order for the deal to close. Examples of closing contingencies include the release of all liens on the practice's assets, successful negotiation of lease assignments or a new lease, and execution of non-compete agreements by all associates.

After both parties have signed the letter of intent, you should be mindful of the "no-shop" clause (if included in the LOI), which means you will no longer be able to seek other offers for your practice. Your practice is essentially "off the market" and committed to this buyer and its process. The no-shop clause may even require you to notify the buyer if you receive other offers or letters of interest from other potential buyers.

The LOI is likely to contain an estimated closing date or a date when the no-shop clause expires. If the buyer fails to close by that date or if the no-shop expires, you can go back to the market in search of other offers. Most often, the DSO will ask for an extension of the no-shop period, and sometimes the no-shop clause will include details by which the buyer can automatically receive an extension. The language of the no-shop clause should be carefully reviewed by your attorney.

Finally, you must keep in mind that the purchase price set forth in the LOI is based on the DSO's estimate of your

EBITDA from the limited financial data it received. Once the buyer completes its quality of earnings review and determines your actual EBITDA, the purchase price may be adjusted if the number is different from the preliminary estimate.

PHASE 2: DUE DILIGENCE

Once a DSO has decided it is interested in your practice, it will conduct due diligence in two phases. The first phase is done before the DSO even issues its letter of intent. During this preliminary due diligence, DSOs typically look at the operations of the practice before they make an offer. Specifically, they want to learn the following types of information:

1. A breakdown of the ownership of the practice. Who are the owners of the practice, and what percentage of the practice does each person own?
2. A management organizational chart. Who has decision-making authority over the practice? Who do the various staff members report to?
3. Financial records for the past three years. This will typically include tax returns and financial statements for the last three years. In some cases, they also request the owner's personal tax returns.
4. Payor mix.
5. Production/collection reports by provider.
6. Compensation structure for associates. How are the associates paid? How are they classified (i.e., as

employees or independent contractors)? What benefits are offered to associates? Do they have written restrictive covenant agreements?

7. Payroll data for staff members.

8. Facility description. What is the square footage, number of operatories, and type of technology used at the office?

9. Lease description and a copy of your lease (if applicable). If you lease, how much do you pay in rent? Do you have renewal options in your existing lease?

As you can see, this is a fairly comprehensive list. And this is just to get an offer.

After you receive an offer, negotiate the terms, and sign the letter of intent, the scope of the due diligence will get substantially more intense. It is basically the equivalent of putting your practice, and every decision you have ever made as the owner, under a microscope and picking it apart into tiny pieces.

As part of their infrastructure, larger DSOs have dedicated teams of people whose sole function is to understand every aspect of your practice. There are operational teams, accounting teams, IT teams, regulatory teams, and legal teams. You name it; they typically have it. Smaller DSOs will often engage outside consultants to do this type of due diligence.

Immediately following the execution of the LOI, the DSO will likely begin its quality of earnings assessment. As discussed in chapter 3, the Q of E is a form of financial due diligence designed to determine, among other things, the exact EBITDA value, payor mix, production versus collections, and percentage of overhead compared to gross receipts by carefully reviewing the quality of the practice's earnings.

You will likely be inundated with long lists of requests from various teams within the DSO, with many duplicative requests. It is not uncommon for three different people to ask you for the same piece of paper, only to have your attorney ask for it again when negotiating your contracts. The process can often feel painful, to say the least.

This is why we recommend preparing your practice for sale in advance. The scrutiny that all of your records will come under will be intense. They will look at every single contractual relationship you have. They will run judgment and lien searches on the practice and may even run searches on you personally. They will look at your bank records, tax returns, and any data they can extract from your practice management software. They will take a deep dive into your financial record keeping and accounting records. They will look at your agreements with dental insurance companies and study your billing and collection practices to be sure you are compliant with regulations.

What the DSO teams are trying to determine is what the practice earns, what it is likely to earn after the DSO acquires it, and the potential for increased profitability post-closing. The answers to these questions are buried somewhere in the data you are being asked to provide.

For example, we have seen situations where the practice had been coding a procedure incorrectly. The DSO then calculated what should have been collected for all those procedures and adjusted the revenue and profitability calculations accordingly, knowing that, following the closing, it would properly code and bill for that procedure.

By the conclusion of the due diligence process, the DSO will have uncovered every detail about your practice. It will ensure that all licenses are up to date and will know whether or not you and your associate dentists and hygienists are in compliance with CE requirements. It will calculate how much working capital is in the practice, how much debt must be settled at the closing, what your accounts receivable are, and how collectible they should be. These will all become important details in the final deal, as money is allocated in various directions.

We counsel our clients to be prepared for this phase of the process. Very often, the selling dentist will get what we call "deal fatigue" because the due diligence is so tedious and seems to go on endlessly. This is a completely normal and expected feeling, but it does end. In most cases, when you reach a successful conclusion, the end result is worth all the work.

Remember, the DSO wants to do the deal. It does not want to waste its time, resources, and money looking at practices it does not believe are good acquisitions. What the DSO does not want is to overpay for the practice or inherit an unexpected liability or problem. The DSO is offering a multiple based on accurate numbers and on terms that give it comfort and protection from liability. Remember, every DSO is going to put you through a strenuous due diligence process.

Material issues that arise with one DSO are not likely to be avoided by going with an alternate DSO.

If this transaction is what you want for your future, then there is no avoiding the due diligence process and the adjustments the buyer will inevitably require. At this point, the final negotiation will take place, and you must decide if the deal works for you or not. If you have proper legal guidance throughout the transaction, you will have an additional level of confidence that the transaction is being handled properly and you are being protected and getting the best deal possible.

PHASE 3: CONTRACT NEGOTIATION

Following the completion of the quality of earnings analysis, the DSO will direct its legal team to prepare the contracts for the sale. The negotiation of these contracts will take place while the DSO teams complete their due diligence on the practice.

The specific documents that are produced in each transaction will vary based on the particular facts agreed to in the letter of intent. However, the key documents will generally include the following:

- Asset Purchase Agreement(s);
- "Partnership" Agreement for Rollover Equity;
- Management Services Agreements (which typically consist of one key management document and several ancillary documents, such as a license agreement,

equipment use agreement, billing services agreement, marketing services agreement, management services subcontracting agreement, clinical director agreement, and power of attorney); and

- Post-closing Employment Agreement(s).

Asset Purchase Agreement(s)

The vast majority of practice acquisitions are structured as a sale of the practice's assets rather than a sale of the equity of the practice entity. The asset purchase agreement (commonly referred to as an "APA") is the primary sale document. In most cases, there are actually two APAs. One is an agreement in which the DSO agrees to buy the non-clinical assets of the practice (i.e., equipment, intellectual property, physical assets, and goodwill) and a second agreement in which a professional entity (a practice entity owned by one or more licensed dentists) agrees to buy the clinical assets of the practice (e.g., the patient list).

Most of the business terms agreed upon in the LOI will be set forth in the APA in much greater detail, including, but not limited to, a description of the assets being purchased, purchase price and payment terms, directions for the completion of work-in-progress, methodology for the collection of accounts receivable, representations of the selling dentist about the pre-closing operation of the practice, restrictive covenants, documents required to be delivered at closing, transition obligations, corrective treatment obligations, closing contingencies, and indemnification.

Partnership Agreement for Rollover Equity

The term "partnership agreement" is being used here generically to refer to an agreement between the owners of a business. In legal terms, an actual "partnership agreement" is only used when the business is, in fact, a partnership. These are typically designated by the letters "GP," "LP," or "LLP" after the name of the business.

If the business is a limited liability company ("LLC"), or in some states, a professional limited liability company ("PLLC"), the agreement between owners is called an "operating agreement." If the business is a corporation (designated by "Inc.," "Corp.," "PA," or "PC"), the ownership agreement is referred to as a "shareholders' agreement."

If you are receiving rollover equity as part of your consideration for the sale of your practice, that equity will be subject to the terms of a partnership agreement. In most cases, the partnership agreement is a non-negotiable document. It governs all of the owners of the DSO; therefore, most DSOs are reluctant to make any material changes to the document for fear of (1) setting a precedent for future sellers and (2) having to track your unique situation. Similarly, if you are receiving equity in a sub-DSO, the partnership agreement used for the sub-DSO is probably identical to the form used for the DSO's other sub-DSOs. Despite their purported non-negotiability, we have been very successful in negotiating certain strategic provisions by requesting that they be put in a "side letter" agreement, thereby avoiding the need to actually revise the partnership agreement.

Partnership agreements generally cover the following issues: the purpose of the company, names and ownership interests of the owners, voting rights of the owners, names of the managers/officers, responsibilities of the managers/officers, rights of the minority partners (if any), liability protection and indemnification rights, meeting requirements, capital contributions and capital calls (if any), allocation of net profits and losses, timing and priority of profit distributions, transfer restrictions, drag-along rights, dissolution provisions, restrictive covenants, and dispute resolution.

When reviewing the partnership agreement, it is important to understand the risks involved in making an investment in the business. For an overview of the risks associated with rollover equity, see the section labeled "Rollover Equity" in chapter 3.

Management Services Agreement

The management services agreement is a contract between the practice entity and the DSO. This agreement details each of the management services that the DSO will provide to the practice and the fees the practice will pay to the DSO in exchange for those services.

Each DSO's management services agreement is different, but they all cover the same basic services, including staff management, staff hiring and firing, marketing, budget preparation and financial reporting, office policies and procedures, payroll, IT services, record keeping, operational support, billing and collections, and leasing.

Since you are selling the practice, you may be wondering why this agreement matters to you. After all, it is not your responsibility to pay the management fee. While that is true, this document is particularly important if you are holding rollover equity (whether in a DSO or sub-DSO) because it has a direct impact on the practice's bottom-line profit, in which you are entitled to share. Also, in some states, management services agreements may include restrictive covenants that are binding on the doctors of the practice. It is important to review this agreement with your attorney to understand how it may affect you, your financial investment in the DSO or sub-DSO, and your rights as a practitioner after the sale.

Post-closing Employment Agreement(s)

In almost all cases, the selling doctor will be required to continue working at the practice for some period of time after the sale. As an associate of the practice, you will be required to sign an employment agreement. The key elements to take notice of when reviewing your post-closing employment agreement are:

- What is the length of the term?
- How much prior notice is required to terminate the agreement?
- What are the penalties for terminating your employment prior to the end of the term or failing to provide the required notice? (You may lose equity or have other adverse consequences.)
- Will you receive a minimum base salary or a straight percentage of your services? If paid on a percentage, is it based on your collections or your production? How are your collections or production defined (i.e., net of labs or other costs)?
- What benefits are being offered (e.g., health insurance, 401K, CE reimbursement, vacation time, licensing fees, membership dues, etc.)?
- Who pays for malpractice insurance?
- How long is the non-compete, and how is the restricted area defined?
- How is termination for "cause" defined?
- Can you be terminated without "cause"?

In addition, if you have associates working at the practice, the DSO may ask them to sign new employment agreements or, if the existing agreements are acceptable, they may choose to assume your agreements. This is why it is important to have your associate agreements buttoned up prior to looking for a buyer for your practice. Trying to convince your associate to sign a new agreement immediately prior to closing can be difficult. We have had a number of clients who (for good reason) did not want to tell their associates about the transaction until just prior to the closing. When they ultimately approached the associates about signing new employment agreements, the responses were less than favorable. In one case, the associate forwarded the new contract to her attorney, who waited three weeks to provide comments, ultimately delaying the closing by a month. In another case, the associate demanded a signing bonus, and the selling dentist had no choice but to pay it. In each of these cases, the selling dentist did not have a good employment agreement with the associate prior to the closing, and therefore, was unable to simply assign that document to the buyer at the closing, which would have spared the selling dentist a great deal of time, money, and stress.

The decision about when to inform your staff about a pending sale is a tough one. On the one hand, you do not want to create unnecessary fear and panic, which sometimes happens when employees hear about a change of ownership. On the other hand, you do not want to catch them completely off guard by waiting until the last minute because this tends to create a feeling of betrayal, dishonesty, or lack of transparency. You want the staff to feel valued and appreciated. In most cases, the DSO wants to retain the staff after the sale. Your office staff may be the most valuable part of your practice. To a DSO that is spending a lot of money to acquire a practice, staff continuity is key. A dental practice without experienced personnel has very little value.

The best course of action is to work directly with the DSO's transition team to create a reasonable timeline for notifying the staff and transitioning the retained employees. An experienced DSO will have a very specific process for how this should be handled. If you are uncomfortable with any part of the transition plan, the DSO typically will work with you to make the required adjustments.

In our experience, most staff members are happy about the transition once they fully understand the process and realize that the change in ownership will have no adverse impact on their daily working life. For the most part, DSOs do not make drastic changes to the internal management and culture of the practice, but they do, in some instances, add perks and benefits that were not offered while the practice was privately owned.

* * *

Contracts are often presented as substantially final with very little ability to negotiate changes. During the course of our negotiations with DSOs, we often hear things like "We never agree to that," "That's impossible," or "We require this from all of our doctors." Often such rhetoric is simply "posturing." Typically, if a deal issue is important to our client, we can find a way to negotiate and find an acceptable middle ground with the buyer and its counsel.

We are keenly aware that many deal terms have serious, long-term implications and emphasize that with our clients. Whether the issue gets worked out as a compromise or placed in a separate side letter agreement, we can typically find a solution for every problem.

PHASE 4: CLOSING

These days, the actual "closing" of a transaction tends to be a bit anti-climactic. Years ago, the closing was a major event. Everyone would meet in a large conference room. The practice owners would be there with their legal advisors. The DSO's business acquisition team would fly into town with their attorneys. If a broker was involved, he or she would surely attend. The whole team would gather around a large conference table, and there would be stacks of legal documents everywhere. The lawyers would be dressed in formal attire, and they would have each contract properly tabbed and color-coded. The documents would be passed around the table for each person to sign multiple copies, and once everything was executed, there would be handshakes and congratulations all around. Oftentimes, after the signing, the parties would then share a celebratory meal. It was basically a ceremonial "rite of passage" followed by a party of sorts.

Today, we close "on the papers." This means that in the days leading up to the closing, the lawyers will circulate the various closing documents among the parties electronically.

All executed documents are then held in escrow until the closing date. On the actual closing date, the seller, the buyer, and their respective attorneys get on a closing call, which usually lasts about fifteen minutes. The lawyers each agree that all closing contingencies have been satisfied; they agree to "release the wires" (distribute the purchase price to the seller by wire transfer) and agree to release the signature pages declaring everything as final. Everyone says "Congratulations," and the call ends. If you want to have a celebratory dinner and pop some champagne, which was a fundamental part of the deal culture of years past, you are more than welcome to – but don't expect it to happen automatically. Closing "on the papers" is admittedly a bit cold, and we still have fond memories of the "old school" way of closing deals. Technology advances have made the process more efficient and less expensive, but it does eliminate some of the excitement of an in-person celebration. At the end of the day, you still get your payday, and most selling doctors find that to be enough satisfaction.

CHAPTER SIX

Life after Sale

One of the most important things to think about when considering a sale to a DSO is what your life will be like after the deal closes. To best illustrate this, we interviewed four clients and asked them questions about life after the sale. These are true-life stories of clients who sold their practices to DSOs; however, some of the specific details have been fictionalized to protect their identities.

CASE STUDY #1

Question: Tell us a little bit about your practice prior to the sale.

Answer: I was the sole owner of my oral surgery practice. At the time of the sale, I had fourteen locations, and my biggest struggle was recruiting talented surgeons to work in (and frankly, manage) the different practice locations. I was also the largest producer of all my doctors. I worked very long clinical hours and spent my evenings and weekends dealing with the managerial aspects of being the owner of a multi-million-dollar business.

Question: Why did you decide to sell?

Answer: I love what I do, but I was tired. Every day felt stressful, and I knew I could not maintain this pace indefinitely. I also have a young family, and I was looking for a better quality of life. I considered selling a minority interest in the practices to a few of my associates, but I knew I would remain responsible for the bulk of the management duties. When someone suggested I consider a partial sale to a DSO, I knew it was the right time to make a transition.

Question: How did you find your DSO buyer?

Answer: I worked with a broker who was scouting acquisition targets for a newer DSO.

Question: How was your acquisition structured?

Answer: The DSO acquired 60% of my business, and I remain a 40% partner. I am also on the board of the DSO and, while I no longer have the controlling vote, I am still involved in the decision-making process, not only with respect to my locations, but I also participate in decisions related to future acquisitions and organizational growth.

Question: Were there any issues or disappointments following the sale?

Answer: I falsely believed that I would get a break after the sale. That was not the case. I was told that they would hire a new CEO to manage my locations, which they ultimately did, but it took several months. In the meantime, my work hours (and my stress level) pretty much remained the same. Once the new CEO started, I did feel some relief on the operational side, but I am still running the entire clinical aspect of the business.

Question: Did the DSO make any substantial changes to the practice?

Answer: Not at all. Other than some minor changes in employee benefits, the day-to-day operation of the practice remains the same. They also retained all of my staff, so we are still operating with the same team of people.

Question: If you could do it all over again, would you do anything differently?

Answer: I could have done a better job with my associate agreements. Prior to the sale, our surgeons were classified as independent contractors, and that enabled them to run a lot of their own expenses through their own entities. This resulted in a greater financial benefit to those doctors. The DSO required that each of the associates sign new agreements at the time of sale that included a reclassification to W-2 employment and a five-year minimum commitment. Needless to say, the associates were not too excited about this, and I had no leverage to encourage them to sign these new agreements, which essentially resulted in them making less money. In the end, I paid signing bonuses to most of my associates and had to share a portion of my equity with some of the key producers.

Question: What advice would you give to a fellow doctor considering a DSO sale?

Answer: If you are considering retiring within the next five to ten years, then a DSO sale is a good idea. If you plan to work for more than ten years, it is too soon. Being a business owner has many financial and tax benefits that you lose when you sell your business. These concessions make sense if you are working on a retirement strategy, but if you still have more than ten years left, it is not worth losing the benefits of business ownership. Even if you remain a partial owner in the practice, the DSO will not likely allow you to expense the types of things you previously ran through the practice. A sale to a DSO can be a wonderful choice, but the timing must be right.

CASE STUDY #2

Question: Tell us a little bit about your practice prior to the sale.

Answer: I was the sole owner of a single-location general dentistry practice in a large city. I had two associates who produced so much dentistry that I was able to cut my schedule to only a few days per month. When I decided to sell the practice, I was living out of state and commuting to work about four days per month.

Question: Why did you decide to sell?

Answer: My time outside the office made me realize that there were other things I wanted to do with my life. I enjoy teaching and traveling. I enjoy business management but had very little interest in continuing to practice clinical dentistry. So, I decided it was time to make a major life change.

Question: How did you find your DSO buyer?

Answer: I interviewed several brokers and ultimately selected one that found me five potential buyers. After supplying some initial financial data, I received four written offers. One offer had a multiple that was substantially higher than the rest. That is the one I chose.

Question: How was your acquisition structured?

Answer: The DSO acquired 80% of my practice, and I retained a 20% interest in the sub-DSO. I also signed a five-year employment agreement, but I was able to maintain my current schedule of four days per month. My buyer did not have a friendly dentist in my state, so I remain the owner of the clinical entity. When I retire, I will sell the clinical entity to my associate, and she will become the new friendly dentist.

Question: Were there any issues or disappointments following the sale?

Answer: Most of my disappointments happened prior to the sale. I was acquired by a new DSO who planned to close on seven acquisitions, all on the same date. It did not work out as planned. They had issues with their financial backer, and this caused multiple delays in the process. The good news was that they offered the highest purchase price. The bad news was that I continued to own my practice for six months longer than I anticipated while they worked out all the kinks.

There were additional issues after the sale. They did not have their banking and payroll set up correctly, so transferring the employees over to a new system took several weeks. They also tried to change several of our internal procedures, which caused a lot of confusion because it was not properly communicated or organized. These days, the practice is operating smoothly, and the staff seems happy. But the first few months were difficult, and I was afraid some of my staff would leave.

Question: Did the DSO make any substantial changes to the practice?

Answer: The only major change was our payroll system. The new system was rather disruptive and confusing. They failed to communicate and train the staff on these changes, and that created some unnecessary upset. The clinical operations have not changed at all.

Question: If you could do it all over again, would you do anything differently?

Answer: In hindsight, selling to a new DSO may not have been the best choice. All my negative experiences were a direct result of being part of the first acquisition. Fortunately, it all worked out for me, but there were definitely some growing pains.

Question: What advice would you give to a fellow doctor considering a DSO sale?

Answer: Make sure you understand your deal completely. Know how long you are required to work. Understand whether you have the option to cash in your rollover equity and how you will be paid. Make sure the DSO is going to allow you to run your practice the way you always have. In my deal, after a lot of negotiation, the DSO agreed that they would not interfere with my management of the clinical practice unless the revenue dropped in two consecutive quarters. So far, they have yet to intervene.

CASE STUDY #3

Question: Tell us a little bit about your practice prior to the sale.

Answer: Prior to my acquisition, my partner and I co-owned our general dentistry practice in the town where we both grew up. My partner was nearing retirement age and approached me about buying him out. I knew I wanted to practice for at least another ten years, but I really was not interested in running the practice by myself. To be honest, I did not really enjoy being a business owner.

Question: Why did you decide to sell?

Answer: I spoke to a few of my colleagues, and one friend told me that he sold his practice to a DSO years earlier. I was shocked. The practice appeared to be privately owned, as it always had been. We spoke for a while, and he educated me on the fact that some DSOs just operate in the background. To the general public, the practice appears unchanged. That is when I knew I was interested in a DSO buyer.

Question: How did you find your DSO buyer?

Answer: My friend introduced me to the DSO that acquired his practice. They came highly recommended, so when they made me a fair offer, I accepted.

Question: How was your acquisition structured?

Answer: My partner and I sold the entire practice to the DSO. He retired six months after the sale, but I signed a five-year employment agreement with an automatic renewal period. That was eight years ago, and I intend to continue working here until I retire.

Question: Were there any issues or disappointments following the sale?

Answer: Not at all. I was relieved to give up my management responsibility. I love being a dentist, and I love my patients. Now I can give them 100% of my attention, and all the back-office work is handled by the new owner.

Question: Did the DSO make any substantial changes to the practice?

Answer: They changed some of our internal billing and processing procedures, and I recall some changes in our benefits. The benefits were better than what we previously offered, but none of the changes really affected me.

Question: If you could do it all over again, would you do anything differently?

Answer: I had no idea there was a way to keep my name on the front door and have someone else deal with the non-clinical aspects of the practice. If I had known, I would have sold sooner.

Question: What advice would you give to a fellow doctor considering a DSO sale?

Answer: If you are not happy with your current situation or you are feeling overwhelmed by the burden of business ownership, it is worth looking at a DSO. It may not be the right fit for you, but you will not know unless you have the conversation.

CASE STUDY #4

Question: Tell us a little bit about your practice prior to the sale.

Answer: I ran a large New York City-based practice with two partners. Two of us were at retirement age, and the other was a younger doctor. It was a combination of fee-for-service and higher-end PPOs. No Medicaid, no capitation plans, and no HMOs. It was a high-end office with twelve treatment rooms and state-of-the-art equipment. At the time of the sale, we were grossing over $8 million out of our one location.

Question: Why did you decide to sell?

Answer: The two senior doctors were nearing retirement age, and we were watching the high valuations that DSOs were placing on practices.

We felt there was a window between our age and the boom in consolidation yielding strong purchase prices. Also, given the size of our gross receipts, we felt the practice was too big to attract a doctor-to-doctor sale, particularly given that we would need to replace the two retiring partners with at least two young, talented, and productive doctors within a relatively short time frame. The senior doctors also had drag-along rights in our partnership agreement, so once we decided to sell, we were able to require the younger partner to sell as well. When he became a partner, we were very transparent about our plan to possibly sell to a DSO at some point, so there were no surprises.

Question: How did you find your DSO buyer?

Answer: We called Bill Barrett. Bill has been our trusted advisor and counselor for several years, and we were in regular contact with him about our plans, the market, our options, his opinions, etc. Bill ultimately helped us prepare our practice and financial materials, select an experienced CPA to get some clarity on our true EBITDA, and then Bill personally introduced us to three different DSOs, all of which produced offers. In the end, Bill helped us choose the right buyer. We saved a lot of money as well since we did not have to pay a brokerage fee.

Question: How was your acquisition structured?

Answer: The deal was 75% cash and 25% rollover equity (all in the master DSO); however, the buyer required a 15% cash holdback. If we meet our revenue target after year two, we get the entire 15%. If we miss our revenue target, we could lose a portion of the holdback.

Question: Were there any issues or disappointments following the sale?

Answer: Not really. Our only disappointment was the loss of all the perks that come along with being a business owner. Transitioning to W-2 employment resulted in a substantial decrease in our overall compensation, but given retirement was only about three years away, we did not let this get in our way.

Question: Did the DSO make any substantial changes to the practice?

Answer: It has been a little more than six months since we closed and, so far, the changes have been relatively minimal. They replaced all of the computers and technology, and we now have regularly scheduled "corporate" phone calls and training that we have to participate in as a group. It has been a mental adjustment going from a privately-owned business to being part of corporate America, but we still run the day-to-day operation and manage all the staff with almost no change.

Question: If you could do it all over again, would you do anything differently?

Answer: Not really. We are pretty happy.

Question: What advice would you give to a fellow doctor considering a DSO sale?

Answer: I have never had to speak so frequently with an attorney or accountant, and it was exhausting and very time-consuming to go through the process. In one of our earlier conversations, I recall when Bill gave us a lecture on deal fatigue, and he was right. We were lucky to have Mandelbaum Barrett on our side because they kept us calm, focused, and informed on the various issues and throughout the process. We now realize how complex and challenging the process is (nothing like the private sales and purchases we previously experienced when we bought a few small practices over the years), and we are grateful for Bill's guidance and his introduction to an experienced DSO accountant. I'm not sure how we could have closed the deal without them.

* * *

Over the years, our clients have shared other experiences about their lives after selling to a DSO. One, in particular, had long-standing relationships with his vendors, and he paid his bills religiously the moment they came in. It was simply how he liked to conduct business and part of the great reputation he enjoyed in the industry. Once the DSO took over, they began paying invoices net sixty days. This was standard operating procedure for the DSO, but it raised issues for the selling doctor. Vendors started calling and asking why payments were coming in late and questioned whether he wanted to continue working with them.

Many of our clients were relieved to be removed from the responsibilities of hiring and firing, but a few were unhappy about the loss of control.

There will certainly be differences in the way the DSO manages your practice as opposed to the way you are accustomed to operating. Loss of autonomy and control is a valid concern. Nevertheless, it has been our experience that once the dust settles, most sellers find that working with a DSO teaches them a different skill set and often improves their management and leadership abilities.

CHAPTER SEVEN

Affiliating with Other Practices

Although very few professionals have been able to do it successfully, recently, we have leveraged our decades of experience, representing hundreds of dentists and dental specialists throughout the country, to join together several doctors into an "affiliation" or "affiliate group" for the purpose of a collective sale to a single buyer. This approach is predicated on the concept that the larger the EBITDA the DSO will acquire, the higher the potential multiple they will offer. In other words, a larger EBITDA means a greater multiple, which means a greater purchase price for each seller participating in the group sale.

We have utilized this concept to band together several practices as a single combined group seeking a collective sale. This "affiliation" or "affiliate group" endeavors to execute upon a group sale and aggregate their EBITDA to attract a materially higher valuation. To illustrate: Imagine ten dentists who are all friends and live in the same general geographic region but do not compete directly with each other. They each generate between $2 and $5 million in annual production, collectively grossing $40 million in revenue, and their combined EBITDA reaches $10 million. In the current market, if they were to sell their practices individually, each might get somewhere between five and seven times their respective EBITDA. However, if they were to form an affiliate group and sell collectively, they are likely to get a 7.5 to 9.5 multiple on their EBITDA. For a practice that has $1 million of EBITDA, that is an additional $2 to $4 million in purchase price. Needless to say, that is a substantial difference and a compelling reason to take a hard look at this option.

An affiliate group like this can be appealing to the right DSO because it gives the DSO a boost in its overall EBITDA and may cover an extensive or strategic geographical marketplace with the closure of one deal. One of the biggest challenges a DSO faces is identifying practices that fit its model. An affiliation can be attractive to a DSO because it presents an entire group of practices at one time and eliminates the need for additional scouting.

Creating an affiliate group is not an easy task. The participating practice owners must make many decisions along the way that require unanimous agreement to move forward. Before formalizing an affiliate group, the potential participants must make sure their practices do not compete with each other. These practices cannot be physically situated near each other unless, of course, there is an opportunity to combine them into one location. There can be little to no overlap in the primary geographic area where the practices attract patients.

It is usually more appealing if the group is similar in culture, fit, and philosophy (e.g., if all of the participants are general practitioners, oral surgeons, or orthodontists; or all participants share another trait, such as possessing a similar make-up of payors).

It is usually beneficial if all of the members have the same retirement horizon. This tends to work itself out as younger dentists are often not ready to sell and might not consider joining an affiliate group. The affiliation model typically works best for practitioners who are five to ten years from retirement. However, this model could work with groups whose members have other demographics—there would simply be different considerations for the group's "end game."

Once the group is assembled, the due diligence phase can begin. Each practice must look closely at its financials, valuation, and individual EBITDA to assess what it brings to the table. This is valuable even if a practice owner ultimately decides not to participate, but it is essential if the owners wish to combine their collective EBITDA.

Ideally, a group of doctors forming an affiliate group will use one common accounting firm that is not only experienced in dentistry and industry consolidation but also has the bandwidth to recast the practices' financials quickly and the expertise to determine their profitability by applying the same methodology to each practice. This requires converting financials from a cash basis to an accrual basis and "normalizing" the practices' earnings through an "add-back" analysis. The result of this exercise is to create a uniform package to present to the prospective DSOs in a standard format that conforms to their valuation approach. This financial analysis is sometimes referred to as a "sell-side quality of earnings" study or review.

It is critical to prepare the "sell-side quality of earnings" early because one or two of the potential members may find that their EBITDA is lower than they imagined, and they might not be willing to sell for that reason. Having a template whereby each member of the affiliate group agrees to be evaluated in the same way will make a difference to a DSO and can also equip the selling doctors with knowledge and understanding of a fair valuation. Participants need to go into the affiliate group with a solid understanding of their individual valuation and profitability. The accounting firm will review financials from the past three years, making adjustments until there is a consistent measurement of the value of the practices.

We also recommend that the affiliate group obtain background checks and judgment and lien searches on all participants. This is the time for full disclosure, first among all participants of the group and later with the interested DSOs. It is only fair that all of the participants in the group know whether any of the participants have "warts" that could jeopardize the viability of a DSO deal.

Once each participant has a clear sense of his or her EBITDA, there are several things the group needs to agree upon and memorialize in a formal, binding "affiliation agreement."

First, everyone must agree to sell once an offer is accepted. One or two members cannot decide to bail out if they change their minds to the detriment of the others. This requires that everyone agree in advance on an acceptable range for the multiple offered by a DSO, as well as to several other material business and financial terms. All participants must also agree on what percentage of the total enterprise value will be allocated to rollover equity, holdbacks, and earn-out terms that may be part of the deal. The participants must also agree on how long they are willing to be employed by the DSO after the closing.

Participants should consider how they will decide to accept an offer. Will they require a majority vote or a unanimous vote? It is up to the group to determine these parameters, but this must be worked out and memorialized in the affiliation agreement prior to soliciting offers.

We do not recommend that any one participant have the power to hold up a deal. A DSO may have an issue with one of the practices in the mix and may ask to have it removed from the group sale. Reasons for removal could be the location or size of the office, its proximity to an existing location of the DSO, a regulatory or due diligence concern, or an issue with one of the practitioners. If this occurs, that practice owner must be willing to drop out of the group.

We recommend that the participants set parameters in advance for a situation like this as a precautionary measure. For example, if there are ten practices in the affiliate group, the affiliation agreement might require the DSO to accept at least eight of them, or the affiliation terminates. The participants do not want to be in a position where the DSO rejects enough of the practices that it pushes the group's total EBITDA down to a lower multiple, thereby defeating the purpose of the affiliation. The more key terms the participants agree to and anticipate ahead of time, the easier it will be to attract and negotiate with potential DSO buyers.

Keep in mind that the participants are not creating a new corporation or business entity with this approach; instead, they are affiliating with like-minded doctors to create a more substantial acquisition target for the buyer. However, there are three things needed for certain. First, the affiliate group will need a law firm familiar with and experienced in this unique strategy (and to our knowledge, there are very few in the United States who have successfully done this). Second, the affiliate group will need a sophisticated accounting firm with experience, size, and bandwidth to recast years of financials for several practices simultaneously. Third, the affiliate group must have a formal agreement among all participants outlining the parameters for sale, including voting rights, termination rights, and the responsibilities of each participant in the affiliate group.

Selecting a law firm and an accounting firm to represent the affiliate group is a crucial step. After the DSO makes its offer and is accepted by the affiliate group, each practice will be presented with an individual purchase agreement and other ancillary transaction documents. If each group participant has its own counsel reviewing and negotiating the deal documents, the DSO will receive ten different sets of revisions and will quickly become frustrated and disillusioned, thereby jeopardizing the deal for everyone. However, if the participants agree to use the same law firm and accounting firm, the negotiation process is far more efficient, thereby saving all participants time and money while affording everyone a better chance of success to reach the desired outcome.

The right law firm and accounting firm should be able to assist the group in identifying potential buyers and present the affiliation data for consideration. In our experience, DSOs are eager to look at these packages when we present them because of the relationships and reputation we have built over time and the way in which we organize the information and present each practice to the market.

In addition, the law firm could approach a private equity firm that is looking to invest in dentistry but has yet to develop the business. A significant acquisition could be a way to launch into the space and begin building out its infrastructure by acquiring several locations on the first closed deal.

Entering into an affiliation can be a great strategy for selling your practice and extracting a much higher purchase price than you otherwise might expect as an individual seller, but this approach can get derailed very quickly if details are not worked out in advance.

One of the biggest challenges is finding the right participants for a group and coming to an agreement on the myriad of terms typical in sales of this type and size. There must be a high element of trust among the participants, as they will be sharing sensitive financial information with one another and commingling the fate of their professional futures with the others' practices.

If the thought of an affiliation sounds appealing to you, it might be time to have dinner with a few choice friends.

CHAPTER EIGHT

Creating Your Own DSO

One of the most common questions we receive from clients is, "Should I form my own DSO?" If you consider yourself an entrepreneurial dentist and have no immediate desire to sell your business, creating your own DSO may give you the competitive advantage you need to grow and scale your organization. Also, if you are not a licensed dentist but recognize that the dental industry can be very profitable, a DSO may be a great opportunity for you to get into the game.

WHY CREATE A PERSONAL DSO?

In this section, we will discuss the two most compelling reasons you may consider creating a personal DSO.

Reason #1

First, you may wish to bring on a non-licensed partner or investor, or perhaps you want to allow a staff member to own a portion of the business. As discussed in chapter 1, most states prohibit a non-dentist from owning a dental practice. DSOs are not dental practices. They are management companies, and as such, they are not governed by the same ownership restrictions.

For the most part, anyone can own an interest in a DSO. The DSO will collect management fees from the practice, and the non-licensed owner(s) will share in the DSO profits.

If you are thinking about forming a DSO and you are not a dentist, your success will likely depend on partnering with a licensed doctor whom you trust. That is not to say that you must give the dentist an equity stake in your DSO (although that is often our recommendation), but you will need a dentist on your side to make the business model work practically as well as from a legal and regulatory perspective. Keep in mind that you cannot buy the practices through your DSO entity. You will need a "friendly dentist" to purchase the clinical assets.

Let's review two recent examples of what can happen when non-dentists start their own DSOs. The first one involved three investors who heard that a lot of money could be made by owning a dental practice, so they found a dentist to be their partner. That doctor happened to be a periodontist. Together, they formed a DSO and proceeded to buy their first general dentistry practice. The seller was required to sign a long-term employment contract, but it quickly became clear that the seller was not interested in working and was ultimately fired. Unfortunately, there were no other associates at the practice. The periodontist could not work at the practice because he was not a general dentist, and he had his own practice to run.

They were forced to cancel all patient appointments until they eventually hired a replacement associate, which took several weeks. In the meantime, they lost several of their staff members and most of their revenue. The investors had no idea how to manage a practice, and the periodontist was busy with his own practice. The partners recently agreed to wind up the DSO and sell their one location.

Our second example involves a similar investor client who got excited about the opportunity to invest in dentistry after watching a friend successfully grow a DSO. With no knowledge of the dental industry but with a strong desire to learn and a history of entrepreneurial success, he contacted our firm. In addition to setting up his DSO, we also introduced this client to a nationally recognized practice management firm called Fortune Management. Through this relationship, our client was able to get the tools he needed to successfully manage a practice. It also led to an introduction to a "friendly dentist." Our client offered the dentist a 5% ownership interest in his DSO and an employment agreement to serve as his "clinical director."

In short, they are off to an excellent start, doing proper due diligence, making smart acquisitions, and developing a nice range of consolidated services. As in all businesses, it is not just how you do something; it is who you do it with that is important.

Reason #2

The second reason for creating a personal DSO is if you have multiple practice locations and wish to take advantage of certain economies of scale by consolidating and centralizing the management of those practices. Your personal DSO can take over the back-office functions for all locations, including payroll for the staff, leasing equipment, ordering supplies, billing, marketing, scheduling, and the like.

Imagine a scenario where you have five practice locations, each owned by a separate entity for liability protection purposes. Now let us assume you have one employee who works as a dental assistant at three of the five locations. Which practice entity is her employer? Does she get paychecks from three offices or just one? How do you keep track of her overtime and vacation time? Is someone consolidating her hours at each location and keeping track of her accrued benefits? This is just one employee, but if you are operating five offices, there are likely many employees who are shared among the offices.

What if you need to hire a bookkeeper, a marketing consultant, an HR director, or even a chief operating officer or chief financial officer? Which entity will employ these people, and how will you allocate these expenses among the different practices? Centralized management and maximization of fixed overhead lead to greater profitability.

There are two legal issues to keep in mind when it comes to payroll. First, most states require that the doctors be employed by the practice entity and not the DSO. Second, some states also require licensed staff members (including dental assistants and hygienists) to be employed by the practice entity. In those states, we often implement employee leasing arrangements that allow all licensed professionals to be employed by one practice location and leased to the various other locations as needed.

As the owner of multiple practice locations, you may currently order supplies and purchase or lease equipment through each of your individual practice entities. However, consolidating these efforts and allowing the DSO to purchase the equipment and supplies for all of your offices may entitle the DSO to bulk discounts and better payment terms.

* * *

Determining *when* to create a personal DSO tends to be the biggest challenge for our entrepreneurial doctor clients. Creating a DSO comes with a certain level of administrative burden and a cost that must be justifiable. You will need to create a new legal entity, open a new bank account, set up new payroll, and file an additional tax return. In the short run, these steps take time and require a budget for accounting and legal expenses.

If you currently have two locations and no partners, a DSO may sound appealing because of your plans for growth and expansion. It may also be advantageous to set it up now so you have the infrastructure in place as you continue to grow. Although a DSO theoretically sounds like a great plan, a DSO with only two locations is not likely to save much in the way of consolidated expenses, and thus it may be difficult to justify the initial startup costs and the additional administrative burdens. In our experience, unless there is a non-licensed partner/investor involved, most clients choose not to form a personal DSO until they have at least three practice locations.

HOW TO CREATE A PERSONAL DSO

Creating a DSO involves several decisions, almost all of them falling into the legal category. You will need to create one or more new business entities and enter into several agreements between the new management company and each practice entity.

One advantage to creating your DSO before bringing on partners is that, as the founder of the DSO and the practices, you can establish fair and appropriate management fees and compensation. On the other hand, if you try to form the DSO after bringing on a partner, the partner will undoubtedly want to review and revisit your management fees and will have a vested interest in expanding his or her minority rights.

When creating a personal DSO, the first step is to form a new legal entity that will act as the management company. Unlike a dental practice, which is regulated by state law and may be required to be formed as a professional corporation (PC) or professional limited liability company (PLLC), the DSO can be formed as any type of entity. Most of our clients choose to form their DSO as a limited liability company (LLC), which usually affords the greatest flexibility, but it can also be formed as a corporation or partnership. When it comes to choosing an entity structure, there are important tax considerations that must be evaluated by your accountant prior to formation.

If you choose to form a corporation, it will be taxed as a C corporation unless it files an election to be taxed as an S corporation. The income of a C corporation is taxed at both the corporate level and at the shareholder level. In other words, when money flows into the business, it is subject to a tax at the corporate tax rate. Once that money is distributed out to an owner in the form of a dividend, it is taxed again at the owner's individual tax rate. S corporations, like LLCs, are referred to as "pass-through entities." This means that the owners of the business pay tax on the income at their individual tax rates, regardless of whether that money is distributed to the owners. There is no corporate-level tax on S corporations or LLCs.

S corporations have additional restrictions that may present a problem given your particular circumstance. S corporations may only be owned by individuals. If you have a private investor who wants to own an interest in your DSO through an existing LLC, an S corporation will not be an option because LLCs cannot own shares in an S corporation. In addition, the owners of an S corporation must be U.S. citizens, and there is a limit on the number of shareholders an S corporation may have.

Another advantage of LLCs is that they have the option to be taxed as S corporations. We often form LLCs when a business is first getting started, but as the business grows and adds more employees, the accountant may decide that the LLC could reduce its taxes if it elects to be taxed as an S corporation.

Needless to say, it is very important to discuss the "selection of entity" decision with your accountant and attorney prior to forming the DSO.

Whatever business entity you choose, it will be formed by filing a document with the state where the DSO will be located. If you plan to manage practices in multiple states, you will need to register the DSO in each state where it manages a practice so it may lawfully conduct business.

Once the entity has been formed, your attorney will prepare certain organizational documents. The only organizational document required for an LLC is an operating agreement. If you are the sole owner of the LLC, this will be a very basic document designed simply to ensure your liability protection. If you have partners, the operating agreement will be negotiated among the owners and include details regarding voting, management, contributions, distributions, restrictive covenants, and buy-sell terms.

If your DSO is formed as a corporation, your organizational documents will include organizational minutes, by-laws, and, if you have one or more partners, a shareholders' agreement. A shareholders' agreement has essentially the same function as an operating agreement. It simply has a different name in the context of a corporation.

Regardless of whether you use an operating agreement or a shareholders' agreement, the following key questions must be answered and addressed in the agreement:

- What percentage of ownership will each owner hold?
- Who will serve as the officers/managers of the DSO?
- What voting percentage is required to approve an act by the DSO?
- Will any decisions require unanimous or super-majority consent of the owners?
- Will the officers/managers be paid separately for managing the DSO?

- Will the owners be required to make additional capital contributions or loans to the DSO?
- What happens if an owner fails to make a capital contribution or loan?
- When will distributions be paid to the owners, and who will determine the amount available for distribution?
- What services will each owner perform on behalf of the DSO?
- What happens if an owner wants to leave the DSO?
- What happens if an owner dies or becomes disabled?
- Under what circumstances can an owner be forced out of the DSO?
- In the event of a buyout, how will the purchase price for an owner's interest be determined?
- Will owners be restricted from transferring their equity?
- Will owners be permitted to own an interest in another DSO or a competing dental practice?
- If an owner desires to acquire a practice or its underlying real estate separately, is that owner permitted to make this investment on his own, or must it be presented to the owners as a corporate opportunity?

Once your DSO is formed and your organizational documents are finalized, the last step is to prepare the necessary management agreements that will be signed between the DSO and each practice under management. Again, if you are the sole owner of the DSO and the practices, the preparation of these documents will be straightforward and an internal function only. However, if you have minority partners, the documents will need to be reviewed and negotiated by all owners.

The exact composition of the management agreements will vary depending on the specific facts and circumstances of your particular DSO. We generally refer to these documents as the "DSO Package." Prior to drafting any documents, we will ask a series of questions to determine which management services will be provided by the DSO, which responsibilities will be retained by the practices, and how the management fees will be calculated. This is also done in cooperation with your accountant, keeping in mind that the law, in most states, prohibits a practice from paying a DSO based on a percentage of profits. Therefore, the management fee should always be stated in terms of a fixed fee. Once we know the specific details regarding the relationship between the DSO and the practices, we can determine exactly which documents must be included in the DSO Package.

The DSO Package will always include a management services agreement (the "MSA"). This is the heart of the relationship between the DSO and the practice. Under the MSA, the practice will appoint the DSO as the sole and exclusive provider of non-clinical management and administrative services.

The exact services will be itemized and detailed within the MSA, which may include, but are not limited to:

- Developing a growth strategy and development of a marketing brand;

- Preparing budgets and financial reports;
- Providing administrative services (including billing and collections);
- Staff hiring, management, and training;
- Leasing non-professional support personnel to the practice (the practice will remain the employer of the dentists); and
- Leasing or subleasing equipment and real estate to the practice.

The MSA will mandate that the practice remain responsible for providing clinical dental services and ensuring that the practice and each dentist hold all necessary licenses, permits, and approvals. The MSA will also include insurance requirements, indemnification obligations, confidentiality obligations, termination rights, restrictive covenants, and dispute resolution provisions.

The management fee provisions within the MSA can vary, but a typical provision will require payment of a fixed monthly management fee, plus reimbursement of all out-of-pocket expenses.

The DSO Package will also include a supplemental fee agreement ("SFA"). Our law firm has invested a great deal of time reviewing the specific regulatory statutes of each state to create a custom SFA that allows the DSO to increase its management fee to account for an increase in practice revenue in a manner that does not violate the law. The SFA sets forth the criteria that the DSO and the practice will follow in determining whether the DSO is entitled to a "year-end bonus" in addition to the management fee stated in the MSA.

Every DSO Package will also include a business associate agreement and a power of attorney. In some cases, the DSO Package may also include a billing services agreement, as well as an employee leasing agreement, and/or a marketing services agreement.

Once the DSO Package is fully drafted and customized for your business, it can typically be duplicated and easily re-used for each practice that you add to your portfolio. Our goal is to make the legal aspects of your DSO formation (and future practice acquisitions) as streamlined and simple as possible so you can focus your attention on patient care and revenue growth.

DSO LIMITATIONS

In 2015, the Attorney General of New York published an "Assurance of Discontinuance" in connection with hundreds of patient complaints filed against Aspen Dental Management, including suggestions that Aspen trained its dentists on how to "upsell" treatment procedures. After a lengthy investigation, Aspen agreed to comply with the state's mandates and guidelines. Most experts in health care regulation agree that this forty-page document now serves as a playbook for DSO best practices. Admittedly, when representing

DSOs, we often refer to the 2015 publication as a reference guide for advising our clients on what they can and cannot do. The following is a general overview of these guidelines:

- DSOs shall confer with the practice owners at least annually to assess the services provided by the DSO.
- DSOs shall not communicate directly with clinical staff concerning the provision of dental care, increasing sales, meeting metric goals, or patient scheduling priority.
- DSOs shall not exercise any control over clinical decision-making.
- DSOs shall not sponsor contests that award or incentivize staff to increase revenue, reduce costs, or sell certain products or services.
- The practice shall have the right to review and approve all policies and procedures that impact clinical and administrative operations of the practice.
- DSOs shall not interview clinical employees without a licensed dentist present.
- DSOs shall not conduct performance reviews for clinical employees.
- DSOs shall not restrict the practice owner from owning, managing, or working for a dental practice in any geographic location for any period of time.
- DSOs shall not restrict a practice owner's ability to retain patient charts or solicit patients.

- DSOs shall not agree to protect the practice against financial losses or assume the cost of employing the clinical staff.
- Practice owners must have full and complete control over their finances.
- All payments to the practice must be deposited into the practice's bank account.
- DSOs may not be paid based on a percentage of the practice's profits or revenue.

Needless to say, the limitations on DSOs are plentiful, and navigating this highly regulated area can be tricky. Our area of expertise is overcoming many of these restrictions in a way that fully complies with existing laws and regulations.

CHALLENGES OF RUNNING A DSO

You will inevitably encounter some challenges in running your own DSO. Most will be the same challenges that all business owners face, which you should already be familiar with as the owner of your dental practice. Some challenges are uniquely tied to DSO ownership. We will identify some of these challenges so that you know what to expect.

As with any dental practice, you will be dealing with staff turnover. In some ways, this will be easier because having multiple offices allows you to move team members around if the need arises. Recruitment will be an ongoing priority to ensure the practices remain adequately staffed.

Some practices will perform better than others. We know of a few DSOs that, among their numerous locations, have one or two of their offices that actually lose money. You will have to dig in and solve this.

You will be dealing with a completely different set of state regulations that govern your DSO as opposed to running a dental practice. These state laws are constantly changing, so it is important to stay in touch with your attorney to ensure your structure remains in compliance with the law. Some states (at the time of writing, Nevada, North Carolina, and Texas) also have DSO filing requirements that need to be monitored.

Recruiting associates is always a challenge, but it is highly competitive in the DSO arena. The larger DSOs have a systematic approach to attracting associates right out of dental school and offer a range of benefits (including student loan relief) for associates who remain with the practice long-term. Therefore, you will have to find a way to be more appealing and competitive in your offer and still find the best people for your culture.

Hopefully, you will be managing a much larger cash flow. You will have a substantial payroll to meet. Capital will always be a concern, and your banking relationships will be critical. This is especially true if you are funding your practice acquisitions with bank loans. Most banks reach an internal limit that often falls short of what an ambitious DSO plan requires for growth. Often you will be signing a personal guarantee on those loans.

As the owner of a single practice, the highest-level employee you may have needed was a practice manager. As the owner of a growing DSO, you may find yourself needing an array of executive team members. You will go from having a controller to needing a CFO. You may grow so large that you need a marketing director, an education director, and perhaps a COO. These are expensive additions to your team but may prove crucial for your continued growth (and sanity).

If you intend to acquire more practices, you will need to establish processes and protocols for conducting due diligence. You will need an accounting firm that understands the taxation and bookkeeping systems that will allow you to keep track of your various entities and their cash flow and expenses. You will also need a law firm that understands (or helps you develop) your successful business model, as well as your growth and retention strategies.

None of this should discourage you. This is what profitable businesses do on a regular basis, and dozens of DSOs are doing it successfully. There is no reason you cannot be one of them.

* * *

CHAPTER NINE

Preservation of Private Practice Dentistry

Throughout this book, we have focused on the corporate practice of dentistry—the concept that a corporate structure can be used to maximize the profitability of practices through outside investors and the consolidation of expenses. We acknowledge the reality that a DSO sale, partnership, or formation is not for everyone. Perhaps you picked up this book because you find the existence of DSOs to be problematic for your business. Or maybe you have felt the pressure to sell but have no interest in doing so.

We believe there still is, and likely will always be, a place for private practice dentistry in the United States, but preserving these practices is becoming increasingly difficult. In this chapter, we will provide some insight on ways that private practitioners can continue to thrive in a DSO-driven industry and can even compete and grow.

Let us take a quick trip back in time . . . The year is 1980 and your father, Dr. James Cooper, just graduated from dental school. From the time he was a small child, Dr. James knew he would follow in the footsteps of his own father, Dr. Paul Cooper. After graduation, Dr. James joined Dr. Paul at his practice, and they renamed the business "Cooper Family Dentistry." For the next ten years, Dr. James and Dr. Paul grew the practice and earned a comfortable living. Dr. Paul retired in 1990, and Dr. James had plenty of money to buy out his father.

You were a small boy at the time, but like your father, you dreamed of becoming a dentist and working with your dad at Cooper Family Dentistry. From 1990 to 2010, Dr. James maintained a profitable practice. He never brought on another associate, never worked more than four days per week, never worked nights, and never worked weekends. He knew everyone in the community and never spent a dollar on marketing or advertising. The office was clean, but the furniture and equipment were dated. The patients never seemed to care.

After graduating from dental school in 2010, you joined your father's practice, bringing a six-figure student loan with you. The cost of education had skyrocketed since your father graduated. For the next decade, you worked alongside Dr. James, but the practice's revenue began to decrease. New dental offices were opening all over the county. Everyone had fancy technology and equipment. Competitors were offering subscription packages and same-day dentistry. Clear aligners surpassed old methods of orthodontics, and practices were treating patients early in the morning, evenings, and on weekends.

By 2020, Dr. James grew tired of the changing industry and decided it was time to retire. Unfortunately, with $350,000 still outstanding on your student loans and having just purchased a new house, you are not in a strong financial position to pay your father the purchase price he is looking for. In addition, you realize that the only way to compete with the other practices in your area is to invest in new technology.

You sit down with your dad to discuss the options.

> **Option 1:** Dr. James could give you the practice as a gift, which would help you financially, but your father needs the buyout money to fund his retirement.

> **Option 2:** You could bring on a partner, which would allow you to increase the hours of the practice and help fund the purchase price for Dr. James's buyout. The only problem is that it will take time to find that person, and you are hesitant to give a stranger equity in your

family business. If only you had hired an associate sooner!

Option 3: You could partner with, or sell to, a DSO. Both you and Dr. James are reluctant to consider this option. Cooper Family Dentistry is your family's legacy, and the idea of "selling out" is not something you are willing to consider.

Now what? The dental industry has changed. You are no longer able to run the practice the way it has always operated. More than anything, you want to preserve the legacy of Cooper Family Dentistry and keep the practice running as a family business. But how can you possibly make that happen in today's DSO world?

If this scenario sounds at all familiar to you, we may be able to help. First and foremost, please recognize that you are not alone. There is a large population of practice owners who are committed to preserving the private practice of dentistry, and it is possible. While DSOs fill a need in the marketplace, particularly in underserved communities, many patients still value their local community dentist. They want a doctor who they trust and has a long-standing reputation in the town. Dentistry is a very personal experience for most people, and this means there will always be an opportunity for individual practitioners.

However, you must be mindful of what occurred in medical practices over the past twenty-five years. These days, approximately 90% of physicians and specialists work for some type of group healthcare organization. While there are differences in the business models (mainly that medicine is primarily insurance-driven), there is a cautionary lesson here. There needs to be a deliberate strategy for the preservation of private practice dentistry.

In order to compete, you will need flexible office hours—mornings, evenings, and weekends. You will also need appropriate advanced technology. Both of these things tend to be difficult as a solo practitioner. For one, most business owners do not want to work multiple evenings a week and every Saturday. For another, if your practice is only open thirty-five hours per week, it will be very difficult to afford the equipment and technology you need.

The following four strategies are the backbone for the long-term preservation of private practice dentistry.

STRATEGY #1: ADD DOCTORS

You cannot do this alone. If you want to increase your office hours, you will need other doctors working at the practice and treating patients. A great first step is to hire an associate. Junior doctors expect to work evening and weekend hours. If a particular associate is not working out, he or she can be replaced with another junior associate. If the associate is great, you may want to offer him or her an opportunity to purchase a minority interest in the practice. You want your doctors to be invested in the success of your business.

Another great way to add doctors to your practice is to partner with specialists. If you cannot afford to bring on a full-time endodontist, oral surgeon, or orthodontist, hire someone to work at the office one or two days per month. This will eliminate the need to refer out specialty work and keep that revenue in the practice. As the need grows, hours for these specialists can be increased.

If you are concerned about the cost of hiring these doctors, there are two things to consider. First, most associates expect to be paid based on a percentage of collections, and those collections are typically net of lab fees. The range for general dentists is typically 28% to 35%, and specialists are usually paid between 35% and 45% of their net collections. This methodology for compensation makes it unlikely that you will lose money on a doctor.

Second, the infrastructure of your practice is a fixed cost. Increasing the number of doctors at the practice will not cause any material increase in rent, taxes, or utilities. It will, however, increase your revenue.

We recommend adding both general practitioners and specialists to your practice. Of course, if your specialists also work at neighboring offices, it is particularly important to have written non-solicitation agreements in place to ensure no one is poaching patients or members of your staff.

STRATEGY #2: CREATE CONVENIENCE

In today's world, consumers only want what is convenient. They want to learn everything they need to know about your practice by visiting your website. They want to schedule appointments online and confirm them via text. Patients want flexible office hours, live chat, teledentistry, and twenty-four-hour call response.

Once doctors have been added to your staff, it will be easier to create this level of convenience for your patients. With a multi-specialty practice, every possible treatment option can be offered, including clear aligners, root canals, implants, oral surgery, endodontics, sleep apnea, pediatrics, and anything else a patient may require.

When you combine the latest technology with specialists working in the facility, a patient can complete almost any treatment in a single visit. Some multi-specialty practices even have an on-site lab to accelerate case completion. Often the efficiency of offering multiple specialties makes it possible to offer treatment at a lower cost and still have greater profitability. Lowering the cost of treatments such as implants, veneers, and clear aligners will attract even more patients and increase case acceptance.

Accepting a wide range of insurance is also a form of convenience for patients. While not every doctor may be credentialed with every plan, offering a variety of insurance and fee-for-service options is ideal.

STRATEGY #3: EMBRACE TECHNOLOGY

Regardless of your personal opinion on technology, there is no denying its appeal to the consumer. We all walk around carrying smartphones, relying on Bluetooth and Wi-Fi to accomplish every task. Patients want to trust their doctors. If you are using dated equipment and technology, you may lose their trust.

Unfortunately, while CAD/CAM, CBCT, and lasers are becoming standards of care and in increasing demand by dental patients, their cost is significant for a sole practice owner. The trend to multi-doctor locations has and will continue to increase in order to allow owners to: (i) take advantage of equipment cost sharing as noted above, (ii) insource high-value specialty procedures, and (iii) promote better utilization of overall practice overhead.

STRATEGY #4: OUTSOURCE

Over the last decade, there has been a substantial increase in the number of vendors servicing the dental industry. These companies allow practices to outsource certain non-clinical elements of the business, such as generating patient reviews, insurance processing and negotiation, billing, and after-hours call handling. These days, you can hire someone to handle almost every aspect of your business.

While it can be hard to decide which items should be outsourced, we do recommend that you consider hiring vendors to assist with those functions you deem important but recognize are not your area of expertise. For example, most dentists are not experts in marketing and advertising, yet certain marketing tools can be lucrative investments for your business. Typically, a business owner does not have time to track the effectiveness of their advertising and can only hope it is working. This is generally a good task to outsource.

Most recently, we assisted with the formation of a new platform called TruBlu Dental Management, Inc. TruBlu is creating the largest platform of technology-oriented dentists with the mission to preserve independent dentistry and private care while unlocking above-market practice growth. TruBlu is focused on leveling the playing field for independent dentists and unlocking profitable practice growth by providing best in class services, solutions, and support. Dentists that leverage the TruBlu platform maintain full equity and operational ownership of their practices.

TruBlu's first offering, TruBlu Plan For Health, LLC, assists practice owners in creating patient membership plans and subscription-based services. These plans are specifically tailored to offer patients a fixed price on certain repeat services (e.g., cleanings and x-rays). The subscription model has been very lucrative in other industries by creating reoccurring monthly revenue. Think about what you currently pay to maintain your Amazon Prime membership or the apps on your phone.

TruBlu's long-term goal is to offer a wide range of additional outsourced services that allow a practice to compete with a DSO without having to sell any portion of the practice. For example, TruBlu Direct, LLC plans to negotiate large-group purchasing discounts and for all their individual private practice clients as if they were part of a consolidated entity. In addition, TruBlu Dental Network, LLC, is forming a network on a state-by-state basis to secure network agreements with the leading dental insurance providers in the US on half of their independent dental practice members.

While many of TruBlu's offerings are still under development, we believe this business model is necessary for the preservation of private practice dentistry and will help give dentists the edge they need to compete with the large DSOs.

If you are still feeling overwhelmed and unsure where to begin, consider hiring a practice management consultant. Many of our clients have substantially increased the profitability of their practice with the help of consulting firms specializing in dental practice growth.

Now, let us circle back to our hypothetical above regarding your family practice, Cooper Family Dentistry. Our recommendation would involve several steps. As a practical matter, you and Dr. James do not want to sell the business to a DSO. What you want is to pay Dr. James for his interest in the practice and allow him to retire. Given the fact that you cannot afford the purchase price on your own, it can be funded in several ways: a bank loan, an earn-out, seller financing, or some combination of these three.

There are dozens of dental specialty lenders that are willing to loan money to dentists even when they have substantial student debt. The bank will want collateral in the practice assets and will also require a personal guarantee, but these lenders do exist, and we arrange introductions to them all the time.

Alternatively, you could pay Dr. James a purchase price based on the future profitability of the practice. For example, if we assume the fair market value of the practice is equal to 75% of the practice's collections, we could structure the purchase price as 15% of future collections over the next five years (15% x 5 years = 75% practice valuation).

Finally, you and Dr. James can agree on a fixed purchase price for the practice, and Dr. James will act as your lender. On the closing date, you will sign a promissory note committing to pay the agreed-upon purchase price, with interest, over a fixed period of time.

Regardless of whether you get a bank loan or agree to an earn-out or seller financing, you will owe money to someone, which means you need to increase the profitability of the practice.

As discussed above, our recommendations are to add doctors (general and specialists), create convenience, embrace technology, and outsource. These are big steps, and you do not need to implement all of these strategies at once. However, if your goal is to preserve your private practice in today's DSO world, you must embrace change.

CONCLUSION

We hope this book has given you a better understanding of how DSOs work and the options available to do business in the DSO universe. As in every other business or profession, there are many opportunities but also many pitfalls. However, with proper guidance and forethought, you can plan your future in (or exit from) dentistry with or without a DSO that is both satisfying and lucrative.

Dentistry is a unique profession, with a wide range of successful business models. It is also a profession essential to the general public, which provides a service too often neglected by the average person. A well-run DSO can provide great service to the communities it serves, as well as stable careers for the many who choose to work for a DSO.

There is no perfect path that suits every dentist. Determining what makes you happy and fulfilled is a critical first step in finding your way in the profession and in life. The maxim, "People don't plan to fail; they fail to plan," rings true in many professions, including dentistry. Our recommendation is to spend some time thinking about which path might work best for you in light of your personal goals, set a professional path forward, and then seek professional help and guidance to execute your vision. Whether you decide to form your own DSO, want to become part of an existing DSO, or continue to thrive in private practice, we hope this book has given you some insight and help in navigating the DSO landscape. With the details provided, you should now have a clear picture of the current DSO marketplace and the opportunities available to you.

We are sure you realize that even though there are a variety of solutions, there are no simple ones. Navigating the complexities of the DSO universe without professional guidance is a risky endeavor. The rewards can be profound and satisfying, but execution is everything, and the "devil is in the details."

As a law firm specializing in providing legal advice to dentists in private practice and to those who desire to enter the DSO universe, we would be honored to provide professional legal assistance to you, whatever you may decide.

GLOSSARY

Add-back Analysis. This is part of a **quality of earnings analysis**. "Add-backs" include deductions or expenses that the potential buyer of a practice will not finance or assume following the acquisition. Some expenses or deductions may be removed entirely (e.g., company vehicle expenses) or normalized based on standard market rates and accounting conventions (e.g., owner compensation, rent, or inventory value). For example, if a practice made a one-time investment in lab equipment, this might result in lower earnings for the year but does not reflect the practice's typical profitability. See also **quality of earnings analysis, GAAP,** and **due diligence**.

Affiliation Agreement. This is the binding agreement all owners forming an **affiliate group** sign prior to shopping for potential buyers. This agreement will typically set out the terms on which the affiliate group is willing to sell, such as the minimum price; post-closing employment terms; the split between cash and non-cash payments; holdbacks and escrows; whether buyers can purchase some, but not all, of the affiliated practices; and how the affiliate group will agree to a sale (e.g., by majority vote). It will also generally include a "drag-along" provision so one practice cannot kill a deal by refusing to sell. It is important to involve lawyers and accountants with experience in selling and evaluating dental practices when creating an affiliate group or drafting an affiliation agreement. See also **cash payment**, **indemnification**, **drag-along**, **indemnification holdback**, and **escrow**.

Affiliate Group or Affiliation. An affiliate group (sometimes called an "affiliation") is when several practices join together as a group for purposes of selling all the practices in a single transaction. The practices in an affiliate group should not directly compete with each other but should collectively serve an extensive or strategic geographical area. Selling as an affiliate group can result in a greater aggregate purchase price than each seller could negotiate proportionately on its own. A DSO may offer a higher price for an affiliate group because there is strategic value in acquiring several practices at once, as it allows a DSO to reduce transaction costs and immediately gain the advantage of **economies of scale** in the geographical area where the affiliate group operates. Prior to joining an affiliate group, the individual owners should get a clear sense of the economics of their practices, usually by determining **EBIDTA**. Additionally, all the owners must agree on certain key points prior to selling as an affiliate group, which are described in an **affiliation agreement**.

Asset Purchase Agreement, or APA. An "asset purchase" (as opposed to an equity purchase) is the most common way to sell a dental practice. The asset purchase agreement is the primary transaction document that sets out all the key terms of the sale. There are often two APAs, one for the sale of the **non-clinical assets** (i.e., equipment, intellectual property, physical assets, and goodwill) and one for the sale of the **clinical assets** (i.e., patient lists, accounts receivable, clinical equipment, and controlled substances) of a practice. The APA will include the purchase price and payment terms for the practice, the representations and warranties of the seller and the buyer, a detailed description of the assets being purchased, a list of other documents and information to be delivered at the closing, as well as other key terms such as directions for the completion of work-in-progress, methodology for the collection of accounts receivable, representations of the selling dentist about the pre-closing operation of the practice, restrictive covenants, transition obligations, corrective treatment obligations, closing contingencies, and indemnification obligations.

Capital Contribution. A capital contribution is the initial investment that the owner of a company makes in the company upon formation. A capital contribution can be cash, services (sometimes called "sweat equity"), or any other type of property (including intangibles such as intellectual property). See also **entity** and **partnership agreement**.

Cash Payment. These are payments made at closing in the form of cash. The most common type of non-cash payment is equity in a buyer's business (see **rollover equity**). Money may be withheld from the cash payment for payment at a later date, subject to a variety of conditions (e.g., **earn-outs** and **indemnification holdback**).

C Corporation, or C-corp. A C corporation is a legal entity that is taxed based on its income, and its owners (technically, "shareholders") are separately taxed for dividends received from the C corporation. This contrasts with a pass-through entity in which profits and losses are "passed through" the entity and reflected on the owners' taxes. Before an entity is formed, consult with a financial advisor regarding entity taxation. See also **pass-through entity, LLC,** and **S corporation**.

Clinical Assets. These are assets of a practice that must be owned by a licensed professional (i.e., a dentist or **professional entity**). The definition of a clinical asset depends on the laws of the state where the practice is located. Clinical assets minimally include patient lists and records and may also include certain dental equipment and controlled substances. See also **non-clinical assets**.

Closing Contingencies. Closing contingencies are conditions that must be satisfied before the sale of a practice is completed. Typical closing contingencies are key employees (especially the owner of the practice) who agree to continue working for the buyer, **due diligence** has been satisfactorily completed, the buyer is able to sign a lease with the practice's landlord (or purchase the property where the practice is located), and all the debts and liens on the practice's assets have been paid off. The parties may negotiate other closing contingencies depending on the nature of the practice being purchased.

Corporate Practice of Dentistry. This refers to the ownership and/or the management of a dental practice by non-licensed investors (as opposed to a model where each practice is owned by a small number of licensed dentists). Since nearly all states regulate the corporate practice of dentistry, the most common way to bring outside investors into a dental practice is through the various **DSO** models discussed in this book.

De Novo Practice(s). A "de novo" practice is a start-up practice built from the ground up in a new location, with no pre-existing patient base or employees.

Dilution. This refers to the reduction (in terms of absolute percentage) of the ownership interest when additional equity in a company is sold to new partners. For example, two owners who each hold 50% of a company may agree to bring in a third owner on equal terms, diluting both original owners to ~33% ownership. Usually, minority owners of a **DSO** or a practice will seek some protection against excessive dilution (such as requiring their consent to sell additional equity or requiring that they be allowed to contribute additional capital to maintain their ownership percentage). Dilution should not always be viewed as a negative event, as it may be necessary to bring in additional owners or investors who can significantly increase the overall value of a company or business enterprise.

Drag-Along Rights. Drag-along rights are frequently included in a business's operating document (such as a **partnership agreement, operating agreement**, or **shareholders' agreement**) and means that the owners all agree to participate in a sale of the business if the majority of the owners vote for the sale. In other words, minority owners will be "dragged along" and forced to sell on the terms agreed to by the majority.

DSO Package. This refers to the suite of documents that governs the relationship between a **DSO** and a practice. The primary document is the **MSA** or **management services agreement**, which is signed with a number of ancillary documents.

DSO. A DSO is a business, separate from a practice, that provides some or all of the non-clinical support services necessary to run a practice for a fee. These support services often include human resources, accounting, billing, leasing, marketing, payroll, purchasing, IT, regulatory compliance, legal, and others. The term "DSO" is an acronym that stands for "Dental Service Organization" or "Dental Support Organization." See also **personal DSO** and **third-party DSO**.

Due Diligence. Due diligence means undertaking a careful investigation of a potential business partner or acquisition target. The most significant due diligence is usually performed by a potential buyer on a practice it is considering acquiring. However, the owner of a practice should also perform "reverse due diligence" on potential purchasers, especially where there are multiple suitors or when the market conditions are favorable to sellers. Due diligence usually includes, among other matters: running **lien searches** and judgment searches on the practice, which can reveal unpaid taxes, debts, or legal judgments; financial due diligence, which includes a careful review of tax returns and financial statements, and usually a **Q of E analysis**; benefits diligence, such as worker classification (employee vs. independent contractor); contract due diligence, which includes a careful review of the practice's agreements with employees, independent contractors, and vendors; and a host of other issues such as legal compliance, ownership history, and the like.

Earn-out. A portion of the sale price that is directly dependent upon the future success of the practice. Earn-outs typically increase as the practice revenue increases and are usually not tied to a fixed dollar amount. However, in some cases, earn-outs are capped. For example, a **DSO** may want to incentivize the seller to continue growing the practice after the closing but may not want to offer additional **rollover equity**. In that case, the DSO may offer to pay the seller an "earn-out bonus" equal to a percentage of the practice's collections over a period of time or a multiple of **EBITDA** or increased EBITDA.

EBITDA. This is an accounting term that stands for "earnings before interest, taxes, depreciation, and amortization." It is a common metric to determine the profitability of a business. To calculate adjusted EBITDA, begin with gross cash received by the practice; subtract legitimate business expenses; then add interest, taxes, depreciation, and amortization; and finally, add "add-backs" (see Add-back Analysis).

EBITDA Multiple. The practice purchase price is often calculated as a "multiple" of EBITDA. For example, a practice may have an EBITDA of $1 million and be offered an EBITDA multiple of 8, resulting in a total purchase price of $8 million. The "market" EBITDA multiple can vary significantly depending on general market conditions, historical performance, the number of practices being sold in a transaction, the area of specialty, and several other factors. Experienced lawyers, accountants, and **practice brokers** will be able to suggest a range of competitive multiples in the dental marketplace when a practice is to be marketed for sale.

Economies of Scale. A **DSO** or an **affiliate group** that manages multiple practices can create economies of scale by consolidating certain back-office operations and creating a stronger negotiating position with vendors. A DSO that manages multiple practices can handle equipment purchases and leases, supply purchases, payroll, employee benefits, marketing, bookkeeping, and other services with only a small increase in cost for each additional practice. For example, a DSO may hire a single professional accountant who can efficiently manage the finances of multiple practices.

Entity. In the context of this book, "entity" refers to a business that has a standalone legal identity, separate from its owner(s). The most common legal entities are limited liability companies, corporations, and partnerships. Partnerships (the least common of the three) are further subdivided into general partnerships (GPs), limited partnerships (LPs), and limited liability partnerships (LLPs). The exact nature of each entity type varies from state to state. To form an entity for the purposes of operating a practice, a dentist, depending on the state, may be required to utilize a "professional entity" that has additional requirements and restrictions imposed both by state corporate law and local dentistry boards. The most common types of professional entities are professional limited liability companies (PLLCs) and professional corporations (PCs, sometimes called "professional associations" or PAs). It is important to speak with an experienced corporate attorney and financial advisors when initially forming any entity for the purposes of operating a business, as there are significant tax and liability consequences for each type of entity.

Escrow. To place something in "escrow" (usually cash) means to give it to a third party to hold and to release only if certain conditions are met. In the context of a practice sale, cash is usually placed in "escrow" to cover potential costs that arise following a sale. For example, a portion of the purchase price (usually 5–10%) may be placed in escrow to cover debts or liabilities, or undiscovered or unresolved claims against the business. Escrowed amounts are usually released to a party after a certain amount of time has passed, provided that no claims have been made. See also **indemnification** and **indemnification escrow**.

Fire Sale. In the context of business transactions, this term refers to the sale of a business by an extremely motivated seller for a price significantly below the historical market price for similar businesses.

Friendly Dentist(s). The term "friendly dentist" refers to one or more dentists who own a dental practice that is managed by a professional management company such as a **DSO**. A DSO that is owned by non-dentists will utilize a friendly dentist in states that prohibit non-dentists from owning a practice entity. See also **practice entity** and **professional entity**.

GAAP. GAAP stands for "generally accepted accounting principles," a set of standard accounting standards agreed on by professional associations of accountants. Larger businesses usually maintain their financial statements in accordance with GAAP.

Holding Company. In the context of a **DSO**, a holding company is an entity formed to own one or more subsidiaries.

Holding companies may be formed for a variety of reasons, including tax efficiency, legal compliance, and/or liability protection. Multiple subsidiaries may be formed for various purposes, such as owning a specific piece of property or providing management services to a specific practice or group of practices. See also **wholly-owned subsidiary**, **master DSO**, and **sub-DSO**.

Indemnification Holdback or Indemnification Escrow. This refers to a portion of the purchase price (generally 5–10%) that is "held back" by the buyer of a practice or placed in "escrow" with a third party to cover the costs of any undisclosed or unresolved liabilities due to the practice's operation prior to the sale. These amounts are typically released to the seller after a certain period (usually one to two years) following the sale, provided no claims are made.

Indemnification. Indemnification is a promise by one party to pay another party for certain damages. For example, the seller of a practice must always indemnify the buyer for damages resulting from the seller's breach of the representations and warranties that the seller makes when selling a practice. Typical representations and warranties made by a seller are: that the practice has been in compliance with applicable law at all times, that the seller is the legitimate owner of the practice, that the seller has the legal authority to sell the practice, that there are no undisclosed claims or liabilities against the practice, that all employees and independent contractors have been properly classified, and many others.

Letter of Intent, or LOI. This is a preliminary document setting out key terms of a proposed business transaction. An LOI is usually non-binding (meaning it does not obligate the parties to complete the proposed transaction), except for a few key provisions such as confidentiality (which might be included in a separate document called a **non-disclosure agreement or NDA**) and a **no-shop or exclusivity clause**. The purpose of an LOI is to ensure that the parties agree on important terms (e.g., purchase price, payment terms, performance targets for earn-out payments, employment terms following the sale, due diligence, and closing contingencies). It is important to have a competent corporate attorney review both the LOI and NDA prior to signing.

LLC, or Limited Liability Company. An entity formed through the filing of a Certificate of Formation or similar document with a Secretary of State. Once formed, the LLC provides entity protection for its owners (or "members"). Some states allow an LLC to own clinical assets and to act as a professional entity, while other states only allow a PLLC or professional limited liability company to do so.

Management Services Agreement, or MSA. An MSA is the primary document setting out the terms by which a **DSO** provides management or operational services to a practice. The relationship is typically governed by a suite of documents referenced in the MSA, including a license agreement, equipment use agreement, a billing services agreement, a marketing services agreement, a management services subcontracting agreement, and others. The MSA describes the overall relationship between a practice and the DSO and specifies the services a DSO will provide to the practice, as well as the payments that the practice will make to the DSO for such services.

Master DSO. A master DSO is a **DSO** that owns one or more **sub-DSO**s instead of owning practice assets or providing operational services directly to a practice. The sub-DSOs then provide the actual operational services and own non-clinical assets of individual dental practices.

Non-clinical Assets. These are assets of a practice that are not required by law to be owned by a licensed dentist or **practice entity**. What constitutes a non-clinical asset depends on state law. Typically, non-clinical assets include some or all of the following: physical assets (computers, office equipment, and sometimes dental equipment such as x-ray machines), real property, intangibles such as intellectual property and goodwill, and some contracts. See also **clinical assets**.

Non-clinical Employees. These are all employees of a practice other than the licensed dentists (and, in some states, the hygienists and/or dental assistants). Non-clinical employees, in contrast to clinical employees, can be hired by a non-professional entity (such as a **DSO**).

Non-compete. A non-compete is a type of **restrictive covenant** that prohibits a party from engaging in competitive activity in a specific geographic area for a specific length of time. For example, a dentist who is selling a practice will generally be required to agree to a non-compete provision prohibiting the dentist from practicing near such practice for a number of years (typically two to five) following the sale of the practice unless the dentist is working for the buyer. Non-competes must be "reasonable" in time and geographic area in all states and are not enforceable in some areas (as of the publication of this book, the most notable example is California). It is also advisable to have associate practitioners sign non-competes when they are first hired by a practice if permitted by state and local laws.

Non-disclosure Agreement, or NDA. An NDA binds one (a "unilateral" or "one-way" NDA) or both (a "mutual" NDA) parties to keep information exchanged with the other party confidential. During negotiations for the sale of a practice and during **due diligence** (or reverse due diligence), a potential seller and potential buyer will be given access to sensitive business information of the other party. It is important to have a signed NDA in place before handing over any of this sensitive information.

Non-disparagement Clause. A non-disparagement clause is a type of **restrictive covenant** that prohibits a party from making certain negative statements about another party. For example, both the buyer and seller of a practice may agree not to make negative or disparaging remarks about each other following the sale of the practice, such as commenting on the quality of the selling dentist's work product or speaking negatively about the experience of selling a practice to the buyer.

Non-solicit. A non-solicit is a type of **restrictive covenant** that prohibits a party from soliciting either the employees or the patients of another party, usually for a set length of time following a transaction. For example, a dentist who is selling a practice will generally be required to agree to a non-solicit provision prohibiting the dentist from hiring the employees of the buyer or marketing to the practice's patients except in relation to his or her employment by the buyer. Non-solicits are not always enforceable, and their temporal and geographic scope varies from state to state.

No-shop or Exclusivity Clause. This is a clause contained in a legal contract between a potential buyer of a practice and the potential seller (typically in an **NDA** or an **LOI**, and almost always in an **APA**, once negotiated). This prevents the selling dentist from seeking out or negotiating with any other potential buyers. Generally, a potential buyer will ask for a no-shop or exclusivity clause before investing significant time and resources into **due diligence** or drafting an APA for the purchase of the practice. This protects the potential buyer's investment of time and resources and gives the buyer additional negotiating leverage.

Operating Agreement. See **Partnership Agreement**.

Partnership Agreement. A partnership agreement is an agreement (almost always written) between co-owners of a business detailing how the business will be managed and how profits and losses will be shared. A well-drafted partnership agreement will deal with key concepts such as **transfer restrictions**, **drag-along rights**, **dilution**, management rights, and others. Entities are more frequently formed as limited liability companies (LLCs), in which case the term **operating agreement** is used, or as corporations, in which case the term **shareholders' agreement** is used. It is important to involve lawyers when drafting and negotiating the initial operating documents of an entity as it is often difficult and expensive to change key management and economic terms later. See also **entity**.

Pass-through Entity. A pass-through entity is a legal **entity** that is not taxed separately from its owners but where profits and losses "pass through" the entity and are reflected on the owners' tax filings.

Personal DSO. This is a type of **DSO** formed by a multi-location practice owner that allows for the centralization of all the services and management needed by the practices for efficiency and minimization of overhead cost. The multi-location practice owner may include additional minority partners at the practice level and/or the management company level. The founder dentist often (but not always) functions as the CEO of the personal DSO.

Practice Broker. A practice broker is one who markets the sale of dental practices. A practice broker can provide several useful functions when selling a dental practice. First, an experienced broker will be able to provide a detailed assessment of a practice and give a fair range for a target sale price. A broker often serves as a "matchmaker" between a seller and buyer of a dental practice due to his or her industry contacts and experience. A broker will charge a fee for these services. Sometimes the fee includes both an up-front fee for a practice evaluation and a percentage of the purchase price (usually 5%–10%) if and when the practice is sold. It is important to do your **due diligence** before hiring any practice broker. Some brokers may also receive "finder's fees" from **DSOs** looking to acquire practices, and incentives do not always align.

Practice Entity. A practice entity is an entity that directly owns and operates a practice (specifically, the clinical assets) and employs licensed professionals to provide dental services. Practice entities are often, but not always, **professional entities**. Practices may be sold to **DSOs** in a bifurcated manner, with a practice entity purchasing the **clinical assets** and **clinical employees** of a practice and a DSO acquiring the **non-clinical assets** and **non-clinical employees** of the practice.

Professional Entity. This is a type of business **entity** formed specifically for engaging in the provision of professional services, such as dental, medical, legal, or accounting. The most common types of professional entities are professional limited liability companies (PLLCs) and professional corporations (PCs, sometimes called "professional associations" or PAs). There are special requirements imposed by state corporate law and local regulators (e.g., the local board of dentistry). Laws vary from state to state but often restrict ownership to licensed professionals. It is important to speak with an experienced corporate attorney and financial advisors when initially forming any entity for the purpose of operating a business, as there can be significant tax and liability consequences to entity selection. See also **practice entity** and **entity**.

Put Option. A put option is the right of an equity holder to require the company to buy back some or all of his or her equity in the company. In our experience, it is rare for a **partnership agreement** to include a put option that would allow the dentist to "cash out" of the **DSO**.

Quality of Earnings Analysis, or Q of E. Q of E is a comprehensive analysis of the quality of a practice's earnings, usually undertaken as part of **due diligence**. A practice's financials are closely analyzed (usually in accordance with GAAP) to get an estimate of the practice's true profitability. Often, a Q of E analysis discounts extraordinary events (such as the sale of property, extraneous deductions, or expenses such as personal cars, vacations, and salaries of family members, and the like). It also normalizes accounting conventions that may cause earnings to appear larger or smaller. See also **GAAP, EBITDA,** and **add-back analysis**.

Restrictive Covenants. These are contractual terms, typically between business partners or between an employer and an employee, that restrict one party's right to engage in a certain activity. Typical restrictive covenants include a non-compete, non-solicit, non-disparagement, as well as confidentiality obligations (see **NDA**).

Rollover Equity. This term refers to an ownership interest in a practice buyer's entity (or affiliate) given to the seller of a practice as part of a sale. Usually, the ownership interest is in either a DSO or sub-DSO and, in some cases, a combination of both. This allows a buyer to put down less cash at the closing and ensures a selling dentist still has some "skin in the game." A seller's agreement to accept rollover equity is riskier than taking cash at closing but can have a higher upside if the DSO is successful. In some circumstances, rollover equity may also be advantageous from a tax perspective.

S Corporation. An S corporation is a legal entity that has made a federal tax election to be taxed as a **pass-through entity** (i.e., the entity is not taxed separately from its owners).

Shareholders' Agreement. See **Partnership Agreement**.

Side Letter. A side letter is an agreement that is signed alongside a primary transaction document such as an **APA** or a **partnership agreement**. A side letter sets out an agreement between the parties for terms that, for one reason or another, have not been included in the primary transaction document.

Sub-DSO. A sub-DSO is a subsidiary of a **master DSO**, formed for the specific purpose of owning the **non-clinical assets** of a single practice. A master DSO may own multiple sub-DSOs and/or directly own the non-clinical assets of multiple practices.

Target Working Capital. "Working capital" or "net working capital" is the difference between a company's current assets (such as cash, accounts receivable, and inventory) and current liabilities (such as accounts payable and other debts). Working capital gives a rough "snapshot" of a company's liquidity at a certain point in time. Target working capital refers to a pre-agreed amount for working capital and is sometimes used to calculate **earn-out** payments or the purchase price of a practice at the time of a sale.

Third-party DSOs. This is one of the two basic models of a **DSO**. A third-party DSO is formed with financial backers for the express purpose of acquiring and/or providing operational services to multiple dental practices. A third-party DSO is owned by non-licensed investors who contract with **friendly dentists** to own the practices that the DSO manages.

Transfer Restrictions. These are restrictions on the equity of a company that prevent the equity from being sold, transferred, or having any restrictions placed on it (e.g., using such equity as collateral for a loan) unless certain conditions are met (e.g., permission from co-owners is obtained). In small

non-public companies like **DSOs,** owners are typically restricted from selling their equity until there is an "exit event"
such as a sale or a recapitalization, or sometimes an investor's
retirement.

Wholly-owned Subsidiary. This is a subsidiary of a parent
(**holding company** or **master DSO**), which is 100% owned
and controlled by the parent.

ABOUT THE AUTHORS

William S. Barrett

Bill Barrett is the chief executive officer of the law firm Mandelbaum Barrett, co-chair of the firm's National Dental Law Center, and the author of the books *Pain Free Dental Deals* and *The DSO Decision*. Over the course of his career, Bill has quarterbacked hundreds of successful dental practice transitions and served as go-to general counsel for prominent dentist-entrepreneurs across the US. In doing so, Bill has been hailed by industry leaders as "a true gift to the profession," "one of a kind," and "a lawyer with the vision to see around corners."

Bill began his career at one of the largest global law firms, headquartered in New York City. After joining the firm in 1999, he was inspired to create a National Dental Law Center, with the objective of setting the standard for the legal representation of dentists and dental specialists in practice transitions. Today, the firm's National Dental Law Center employs the country's leading dental transaction attorneys, and is proud to serve dentists and dental specialists nationwide.

Bill is well recognized as a dental transactional attorney, with expertise in practice sales and purchases, associate buy-ins,

start-ups, and the structuring of management services organizations. He is well versed in the rules and regulations that
govern the profession, with particular expertise in the healthcare regulations governing corporate dentistry and medicine.

Bill has written many articles addressing the legal and business needs of licensed professionals and regularly speaks on
a wide variety of topics to conventions, trade shows, study
groups, and societies, as well as students and residents at
dental and medical schools.

When Bill is not serving his clients, he enjoys coaching youth
sports; fishing; skiing; and traveling with his wife, Jen, and
his two children, Julia and Billy. Bill resides in Mountain
Lakes, New Jersey.

Casey Gocel

Casey Gocel joined the firm in 2008 after
completing her master's degree in tax law at
New York University School of Law. She
quickly became the youngest female partner
in the firm's history and was subsequently
appointed to the firm's executive committee.

As the co-chair of Mandelbaum Barrett's National Dental Law
Center, Casey uses her unique blend of entrepreneurial spirit,
legal expertise, and business acumen to help dentists navigate
through practice transitions, corporate transactions, tax
issues, and estate planning concerns. In addition to bringing

deep expertise to every situation, she is widely recognized as one of the dental industry's most prolific attorneys, regularly spearheading more than fifty transactions each year.

Casey has been named a Top 50 Woman in Business, as well as a Top 25 Intrapreneur. Earlier in her career, Casey was also named one of *NJBIZ*'s "Forty Under 40" for her commitment to professional excellence and community service, one of the "New Leaders of the Bar," and a "Rising Star" by Thomson Reuters' Super Lawyers. Casey lives in Parsippany, New Jersey, with her husband, Dan, and her daughters, Denali and Magnolia.

CONTRIBUTORS

Barry M. Schwartz

Barry Schwartz is a partner in Mandelbaum Barrett's Corporate Practice Group, where he represents dentists in a wide range of corporate matters, including the acquisition and sale of dental practices, entity formations, debt financings and intellectual property concerns.

Peter Tanella

Peter Tanella is a partner in Mandelbaum Barrett's Corporate Practice Group and a founding member of the National Dental Law Center, where he advises dental entrepreneurs through every stage of their growth, including business formation, capital raising, practice sales, acquisitions and joint ventures; as well as contract, employment, real estate and intellectual property concerns. Peter also has extensive experience helping practice owners create succession plans and resolve sensitive matters, including partnership disputes.

Dennis Alessi

Dennis Alessi is a co-chair of both Mandelbaum Barrett's healthcare regulatory and employment law groups, where he helps dentists establish, structure regulatorily compliant healthcare businesses, strike joint ventures and other professional arrangements, comply with federal and state employment laws, and address employee disputes. Dennis also litigates complex healthcare matters in state and federal courts, and addresses matters before administrative agencies and licensing boards.

Philip Mackson

Philip Mackson is an associate in Mandelbaum Barrett's Corporate Practice Group, where he focuses on corporate governance matters, corporate formations, financings, M&A and private equity transactions, and commercial licensing transactions for dentists across the country.

Melody Lins

Melody Lins is an associate in Mandelbaum Barrett's Corporate Practice Group, where she focuses on business entity formation, mergers and acquisitions, joint ventures, commercial transactions and corporate governance concerns for dentists across the country.

Lindsey Priolo

Lindsey Priolo is a paralegal in Mandelbaum Barrett's Corporate Practice Group and a founding member of the National Dental Law Center, where she has worked on hundreds of dental practice transitions across the country, specifically focusing on the acquisition and sale of dental practices, entity formation and real estate transactions.

Daniel Barkin

Daniel Barkin is a partner in Mandelbaum Barrett's Corporate Practice Group, where he represents dentists in financing transactions, corporate issues, practice transactions and practice succession planning.

Cheryl H. Burstein

Cheryl Burstein is the chief operating officer of Mandelbaum Barrett, and a partner of the firm. She concentrates her practice on construction-related litigation and arbitration, and complex commercial litigation for dental industry clients, including business disputes and trust and estate litigation.

"A true gift to the profession of dentistry."
"One of a kind!"
"A lawyer with the vision to see around corners."

SUPERCHARGE YOUR NEXT DENTAL EVENT WITH BILL BARRETT

Armed with candid insights gained from hundreds of successful practice transitions, Bill Barrett educates and entertains conferences, dental societies, study clubs and other professional organizations with:

- Pragmatic advice for dental entrepreneurs at every stage of their career
- Real life stories-successes to emulate and pitfalls to avoid
- Tangible strategies for moving from analysis to action
- Timely intelligence on the evolving dental M&A market

**Email wbarrett@mblawfirm.com,
or call 973-243-7952 for details**